The Physics of the Chernobyl Accident

By

Keith Pearce

Katwab Limited Publishers,
Gloucestershire, UK
Copyright © 2019 Katwab Limited

ISBN 978-1-9164658-1-7

Keith Pearce has asserted his right to be identified as the author of this work.

Preface

On Friday 25th May 2006 I gave an invited lecture at the National Radiological Protection Board's headquarters as part of their Chernobyl 20th Anniversary Seminar. I was the warm up act, giving an overview of the causes of the accident before others gave talks on the dispersion of radioactivity and the effects on the population local to the accident and within the UK. While preparing this lecture I was struck by the range of physics knowledge I was trying to explain and thought then that the accident would make a good backbone to a series of physics and radiological protection lectures or monologues.

In September 2011 I was invited to an International Atomic Energy Agency (IAEA) workshop in Chernobyl to discuss the emergency planning requirements for the site during decommissioning. I and two other invited "experts" spent 3 days in Slavutich and on the Chernobyl site in discussions with their management, safety case team and emergency planners. A great privilege and extremely interesting.

As Head of Emergency Planning for the Magnox tranche of reactors I remained professionally interested in nuclear reactor safety and accidents and was closely involved in the UK's response to the Fukushima events of March 2011.

Now, some years later, I have the time to write some of the ideas that have occurred to me. Can you explain the Chernobyl accident to people who have an interest in physics, but lack reactor physics knowledge, in a way that is interesting and informative?

In preparing this book I've read a lot about the Chernobyl accident. There are still debates about the fine details of the final seconds before the first explosion and even the nature of the two recorded explosions are still debated. What is known is that the operators struggled to manage a large and cumbersome reactor, trying to satisfy the competing demands of the power grid to provide energy after the planned shutdown time, and the desire to complete an experiment on auxiliary equipment. They were working in a society where to be seen to fail at a task could be extremely detrimental to your career and therefore to future access to privilege.

The experiment was delayed at the last moment. During this delay the operators unwittingly took their reactor into a dangerous configuration. It was on a thermal-hydraulic tipping point and a criticality tipping point. Initiation of the experiment bought these together with devastating effect.

In this book I try to explain the physics behind the two tipping points, how the reactor was inadvertently manoeuvred into that situation and what happened next. This book is not an attempt to contribute to the debate about the details of the last seconds. I do not have the expertise nor the data to do that. I'll attempt to describe the contributing factors without judging. In doing this I'll stand with the IAEA who suggested that "*Thus the question arises: Which weakness ultimately caused the accident? There is a second question: does it really matter which shortcoming was the actual cause, if any of them could potentially have been the determining factor?*" (INSAG-7).

Contents

1. Introduction

"An accident has occurred at the Chernobyl nuclear power plant and one of the reactors was damaged. Measures are being taken to eliminate the consequences of the accident. Aid is being given to those affected. A Government commission has been set up."

Soviet Union announcement 29th April 1986, (Ref. 1 and Ref. 2)

1.1. Purpose

There are many popular books about the Chernobyl accident that discuss the failings of the management of the site leading up to the accident, the delay in understanding the severity of the accident, and the acts of heroism and desperation following the accident. There are also a number of learned papers written in journals that argue over the fine points of nuclear physics and the timing of events trying to explain the severity of the accident. The middle ground between these two sets of work is relatively barren. This book is an attempt to explain the physics of the Chernobyl accident to the interested person who is not a reactor physicist. It dips into introductory physics courses to collect the pieces of physics needed to understand what happened and then puts them all together in what is intended to be an accessible explanation of the event.

Inevitably the explanations in this book use a lot of technical terms. I've tried to reduce their usage and use every day English where possible. Important terms are explained in some detail where appropriate. Terms presented in italics are briefly explained in Appendix C.

1.2. A note on references

I have tried to give good references for all of the main points I have made so that those who want to spend more time gaining a deeper understanding of the physics have somewhere to start. Today the internet is a vast store of knowledge or a cacophony of nonsense depending on how you approach it. I use the internet a lot. Wikipedia, now the largest encyclopaedia in history, contains a lot of good material but the quality and depth of its writing is uneven and the editing is haphazard. I use it with care. I often start my search for understanding with Wikipedia but try to remain suitably sceptical and seek other sources as well. As for internet sources for science and the history of science, there are a lot of on-line courses and manuals, some of which are excellent while others less so. The web-sites of expert organisations such as the International Atomic Energy Agency (IAEA) and the World Health Organisation (WHO) are useful, as are industry sites such as the Nuclear Energy Institute (NEI) and the World Nuclear Association (WNA) for example. The internet is dynamic. Pages were there when I referenced them. I cannot guarantee that they will still be there if you look for them.

There is still space in the world of information for good old-fashioned books. I've used several in the preparation of this manuscript.

The approach to take when reading anything is always to consider when something was written, why it was written and by whom. Are they an informed expert or a commentator? Do they have an axe to grind? Were they there? In science, as in most intellectual activities, we value the opinion of others so that work that has been peer reviewed is preferred.

1.3. Setting

The Union of Soviet Socialist Republics (USSR or Soviet Union) was a one-party state with a highly centralised government and economy. Covering Eastern Europe and Northern Asia it included more than one-eighth of the Earth's inhabited land area. It was formed in 1922 and from about 1946 to its demise in 1991 was disengaged from the western world and fighting the "cold war"; a geopolitical struggle between the USSR and the USA and their respective allies. By the mid nineteen eighties, after a period of stagnation, the Union was struggling both technically and economically compared to the capitalist western world. Grand plans were being made to make up the difference, but the ambitious targets were being missed or fudged as often as not.

In 1985 Mikhail Gorbachev become the eighth and last leader of the Soviet Union and launched his programmes of perestroika ("restructuring" in which central control was reduced) and glasnost ("openness" in which the power of the Communist Party was reduced, multi-candidate elections held and media control eased).

Contemporary accounts of the soviet nuclear industry can be found on the internet (see, for example, Ref. 3 & Ref. 4). These, being creatures of their time, glory the current and future achievements of the soviets. Semenov (1983) (Ref. 3) explains that the USSR developed nuclear power for environmental reasons and because their main fossil fuel supplies were in the east and 75% of their population in the west. He makes the boast that nuclear generation would increase threefold within 5 years of the 1983 publication date (one of the grand plans). He explains that the Soviet Union had two main types of reactor; the VVER and the RBMK. The VVER (water-water energetic reactor) is a pressurized water reactor. This is a common design across the world but not the design of reactor used at Chernobyl which was a RBMK. See Ref. 5 for a detailed description of the modern VVER. Details of the RBMK are given throughout this manuscript

Figure 1 Views of Obninsk (Photo K.I.Pearce 21/1/1998)

The development of an alternative design to the VVER[1], namely the channel-type light-water-cooled, graphite-moderated reactors (RBMK) began with the commissioning of the first nuclear power plant in Obninsk in 1954[2]. This was the AM-1 reactor, short for Atom Mirny or peaceful atom. (See Ref. 6 for a first-hand report of this project[3]).

At the time of Semenov's paper, the RBMK 1000 was being operated and built at several sites within the Soviet Union[4]. This design was finding favour because its mode of construction did not require particularly specialist production techniques, unlike the VVER which required very large, high quality, pressure vessels. It is also capable of on-load refuelling which means that it can operate for longer between maintenance shutdowns. Its ability to use low enrichment fuel was also

---

[1] It was, and still is, common for countries to develop more than one type of nuclear reactor at a time. It avoids "putting all your eggs in one basket". In the UK, for example, eight experimental reactors were built at Winfrith in Dorset (Ref. 7).

[2] You can see a film of the Queen opening Britain's first power station, Calder Hall, in 1957 in Ref. 8.

[3] For those interested in the history of nuclear power, the report by Herbert L. Anderson in the Bulletin of Atomic Scientists (Ref. 9) is a very good first-hand account of the programme that led to the first self-sustaining chain reaction in the USA on December 2nd, 1942.

[4] It is common practice to put the electric output in MW after the reactor name, particularly where there are several variants of a reactor type. Thus the RBMK 1000 is a 1000 MW_e version of the RBMK.

advantageous[5].

Plans existed to build 1500 MW and 2400 MW variants of the reactor (Ref. 4). The latter of these was going to be prefabricated in factories and delivered to the site by train for final construction.

The Chernobyl Power station is about 130 km north of Kiev, Ukraine, in the eastern part of the Byelorussian-Ukrainian Woodlands and about 20 km south of the border with Belarus. It is by the River Pripyat (Figure 2). By 1986 the Chernobyl site had four operating RBMK-1000 reactors built between 1970 and 1983 and two more RBMK reactors under construction. Unit 4 had been generating since December 1983. The four reactors together produced about 10% of Ukraine's electricity at the time of the accident.

Figure 2 Location of Chernobyl (Google maps)

The drive, within the Soviet Union, to make economic progress had resulted in ambitious targets being set in many areas including nuclear power. Central demands were to make new nuclear power stations more rapidly and to drive existing ones harder. Failure to meet a target was not an option for ambitious people. Pressure to achieve was intense despite a shortage of labour, particularly of skilled labour, during this period. This led to targets being fudged and poor-quality products being

---

[5] Natural uranium is 0.72% U-235 while most of the rest is U-238. As will be explained later, sustaining a nuclear chain reaction requires that neutron wastage is reduced and that sufficient neutrons are absorbed in U-235 rather than elsewhere. One way of doing this is to increase the number of U-235 nuclei compared to the number of parasitic absorbers such as U-238. Enrichments to a few percent of U-235 are common. See Ref. 10 for more details. The enrichment process took time to develop and was (and is) expensive.

delivered throughout the supply chain. This was felt at the Chernobyl reactor site where there were delays in completing new units. Existing units were generating above their targets but being exhorted to produce even more. A local journalist, Lyubov Kovalevska, published an article exposing a number of long-standing issues at the site a month before the accident (27th March 1986). An extract of this can be found in Ref. 11 (Page 144). It discusses a number of issues about material being supplied to the site late, incomplete and of poor quality as well as poor design specifications, arbitrary timescales and demoralisation of the work force.

About 3 km away from the reactor site was Pripyat, a city with 49,000 inhabitants. 15 km away was the town of Chernobyl which had a population of 12,500. Within a 30 km radius of the power plant, the total population was between 115,000 and 135,000 at the time of the accident (NEA, Ref. 12).

1.4. Introduction to the accident

This section briefly outlines the events leading up to the accident. It uses jargon and technical terms, without which an explanation is nearly impossible. These terms will be explained later. The intention is that when you reach the fuller explanation in Section 6 you will understand it much better. Terms given in italics are defined in Appendix C and explained within the text.

It is normal to shut down nuclear reactors periodically to allow maintenance and inspections that you cannot do while the reactor is at power. In April 1986, Chernobyl reactor 4 was approaching such a routine shutdown. The operators had been ordered to undertake an experiment investigating the amount of useful work you could get out of one of the large steam turbines if the steam supply to it was interrupted without notice. They intended to disconnect the steam turbine from the reactor and perform the experiment just before shutting down the reactor. The experiment had been performed before with disappointing results, but improvements had been made to the control system and they were ready to try again. This experiment could only sensibly be undertaken during a planned shutdown of a reactor. If this opportunity was missed, it would be a while before they had another chance.

Nuclear reactors depend upon the chain reaction to produce energy. In this process a *thermal neutron* hits a U-235 nucleus and causes it to *fission* in which it splits into a number of pieces giving out energy and more neutrons. If you can persuade an average of one of these new neutrons to induce another fission then you have a self-sustaining "*chain reaction*" and the process continues to give out energy at a steady rate. This is difficult to achieve. There are several competing outcomes that can befall a neutron which prevent it from initiating another fission. Without great care there are not enough neutrons to maintain a steady rate of fission and the chain reaction dies away. On the other hand, if you have a situation where more than one further fission results from each fission then the reactor power can increase very rapidly.

During the preparation for the experiment a number of these competing processes that remove neutrons became more effective than usual. The cooling channels, usually a mixture of water and steam, became mainly water. Water is much better than steam at absorbing neutrons so more were lost this way than usual. Importantly the water in the coolant circuit was very near to its boiling point.

The reactor graphite was colder than usual due to excessive pumping of coolant water. This affected the energy distribution of the neutrons in the reactor making *non-fission absorption* more likely. Basically more neutrons were being lost to the reactor structure leaving fewer to initiate the next fission.

Because of power changes leading up to the experiment the reactor was in the middle of a *Xenon transient* which was causing more than usual neutrons to be absorbed by *neutron poisons*, particularly in the middle of the large reactor. Again fewer neutrons to initiate the next fission.

To compensate for these losses of neutrons the reactor's *control rods* were withdrawn further than usual from the reactor centre. In fact, that were pulled beyond the normal operating limits into a configuration now known to be dangerous.

When the experiment started the rate of pumping of cooling water decreased. Because of this the pressure in the cooling circuit dropped and the temperature rose. Water quickly began to boil low down the reactor and neutron absorption in this area was suddenly significantly reduced. The rate of fission increased rapidly and the power density rose in line with it.

To counter this the control rods were released but, because of a design fault and their height in the reactor, they briefly added to the number of available neutrons in the lower regions of the reactor rather than reducing them.

This was sufficient to send reactor power density levels rocketing. Temperatures inside the fuel rose rapidly and the affected fuel pins shattered, smashing their pressure tubes and releasing a steam/water mixture onto the hot graphite. The resulting explosions wrecked the reactor.

INSAG-7, The Chernobyl Accident: Updating of INSAG-1, a report by the International Nuclear Safety Advisory Group[6] (Ref. 13) concluded that "The accident is now seen to

---

[6] The International Nuclear Safety Group (INSAG) is a group of experts with a high level of professional competence in the field of safety. Group members work in regulatory

have been the result of the concurrence of the following major factors: specific physical characteristics of the reactor; specific design features of the reactor control elements; and the fact that the reactor was brought to a state not specified by procedures or investigated by an independent safety body. Most importantly, the physical characteristics of the reactor made possible its unstable behaviour".

A number of design faults came together as the unfortunate result of actions by the operators attempting to complete a disrupted experiment on peripheral equipment.

To understand the power surge that caused all the damage you need to understand the *neutron economy* which determines how many further fissions, on average, result from the neutrons released in each neutron-induced fission. This requires an understanding of the chain reaction and the fates that can befall a fission neutron (a neutron produced by the fission process). These fates depend on the structure of the reactor and the materials it contains and also on temperature. The influence of *delayed neutrons* is also important.

It is also important to have some understanding of how heat is removed from the reactor and how the primary circuit, which consists of the reactor core, the cooling circuit, the steam separator, the turbine system and the coolant pumps, reacts to changes in pumping speed, heat generation and heat removal.

You need to understand the role of control rods and why the reactor's control rods had been withdrawn beyond their usual limits to compensate for void collapse, moderator cooldown and xenon-135 build-up and why that mattered, why their insertion lead to an initial increase in reactivity and why that mattered, why the coolant in the reactor was in a condition where a rapid reduction in density was possible and how these factors combined to cause the power surge that destroyed the reactor.

1.5. Route map

This book provides an outline of nuclear reactors in general (Section 2) and the RBMK design in particular (Section 2.2) and the accident that befell the site in April 1986 (Section 3). It then provides an overview of the physics and reactor engineering required to give a deeper understanding of the event (Sections 4 - 5) and follows that with a more detailed account of the accident (section 6) which you should, having read the book, be better equipped to understand.

Later sections describe what happened following the accident (Section 8).

---

organizations, technical support organisations, research and academic institutions and the nuclear industry (Ref. 14).

Appendices then give more explanation of related nuclear and reactor physics.

2. What is a nuclear power reactor?

This section outlines the basis of nuclear reactor design so that you can understand the later discussion about different types of reactors and the events that destroyed reactor 4 at Chernobyl.

It is important to understand the basics of reactor design to understand the Chernobyl accident.

2.1. General introduction to nuclear power reactors

A *nuclear reactor* is a device which controls the nuclear fission process to produce heat which can be utilised to make electricity, to produce heat for industrial process or space heating, or to provide propulsion for ships and submarines.

Nuclear fission is a process in which a heavy atom is split into smaller pieces. As will be described later (Section 4.2) this produces a lot of heat, a lot of ionising radiation and some radioactive *fission fragments* (sometimes called "fission products").

All reactor designs use the *chain reaction* to ensure that sufficient fissions take place to generate the required amount of heat. In this process a collision with a neutron induces a heavy nucleus to fission giving out heat and more neutrons. If, on average, one of the neutrons released induces another fission then you have a stable fission rate and therefore a stable power level. Reactor control is about managing the fraction of fission neutrons that go on to induce a further fission.

Something is required to keep the heavy atoms in the right place to be fissioned and to retain the fission fragments produced. This is the nuclear fuel, usually in the form of a rod surrounded by a *cladding* to keep it all together, and assembled in a *reactor core*. The fuel itself is usually Uranium-235 (the significance of the number attached to the element name is explained later).

Something is required to take the heat being generated away from the fuel so that the fuel doesn't overheat and damage itself and so that the heat can be used. This is the *coolant* which is usually a fluid that is pumped around the fuel. Common coolants are water at high pressure (so that it doesn't boil), water that boils within the system, carbon dioxide, or liquid metals. Because the reactor produces fission fragments which generate heat as they decay, cooling is required to continue for a period of time after the reactor has been shut down. This *decay heat* can be a real problem when a reactor is damaged or suddenly denied power to its cooling circuits.

Control of the chain reaction is required to ensure that the rate of heat production is appropriate and to enable the operators to shut the reactor down when they wish to. Control mechanisms include:

- doping the cooling circuit with controllable quantities of materials that absorb neutrons (*neutron poisons*);
- adding burnable poisons to fresh fuel (these mop up extra neutrons from the fresh fuel, which is more reactive than older fuel, and are removed as they do so extending the life of the fuel); and
- using rods of neutron absorber (control rods) which can be pushed into or removed from the reactor region as required.

A process is required to take the heat out of the coolant and put it to a good use such as generating electricity or to distributing heat to where it is needed. This usually involves making steam and either using it to drive turbines connected to a generator or propeller or using it to transfer heat to where it is required. If the heat is not removed from the coolant then its temperature will rise and it, in turn, will not be able to cool the reactor.

Figure 3 (From Ref. 15) shows a simplified nuclear reactor system. Note the reactor core where the fuel sits, the pumps which push coolant over the hot fuel, the use of steam to drive a turbine (this diagram is a boiling water reactor where steam generated in the core drives the turbines directly), the generator making electricity when it is turned by the turbines, and the conventional side cooling which condenses the water before it is pumped back into the reactor. Reactors use large bodies of water (seas, lakes or rivers) or cooling towers (as shown here) to condense the water from the turbines.

To learn more about how turbines work look up the "Rankine cycle" which describes the thermodynamic in play in standard power station turbines. (For example Wikipedia (Ref. 16).

It is important to realise that achieving a self-sustaining chain reaction is difficult. So far as we know, it has only happened once in nature (Ref. 17). In almost all configurations too many neutrons are lost by flying out of the reactor or being absorbed in something other than fissile nuclei. To counter this, reactor designers have to carefully choose the size and layout of the reactor and the materials they use to support the reactor assembly and they have to minimise the amounts of non-fuel material used and select those materials that do not absorb neutrons well. This leads to compromises on the strength of reactor cores and their ability to manage thermal and physical shocks.

Two main solutions have been found to produce a sustainable nuclear chain reaction. The first is the heterogeneous moderated reactor (or thermal reactor) in which the fission neutrons are slowed, greatly increasing their chances of inducing another fission. The second solution is to significantly enrich the fuel or change the fuel to plutonium and use fast neutrons to sustain the chain reaction.

Reference 18 gives a good overview of the main types of reactor and provides a table summarising where they are built. Reference 19 gives a full set of statistics about currently operating and decommissioned reactors around the world.

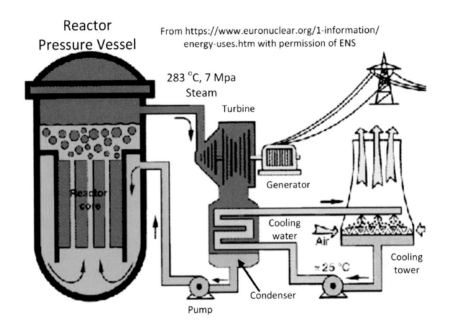

Figure 3 Simplified nuclear reactor

2.2. Outline of the RBMK design

Unit 4 at Chernobyl was an RBMK type of reactor (Reaktor Bolshoy Moshchnosty Kanalny, high-power channel type reactor). This consists of a large graphite pile, 7 m high by 12 m wide. This is almost 3 times the volume of a standard squash court which is 5.64m (high) x 9.75m x 6.4m. This is a large reactor but by no means the largest in use (Figure 4).

The RBMK reactor core consists of a graphite block structure with an array of vertical channels. Most of these channels contain zirconium alloy pressure tubes which contain the zirconium-alloy clad uranium-dioxide fuel. Other channels are for control rods and reactor instrumentation. A refuelling machine allows fuel bundles to be changed without shutting down the reactor.

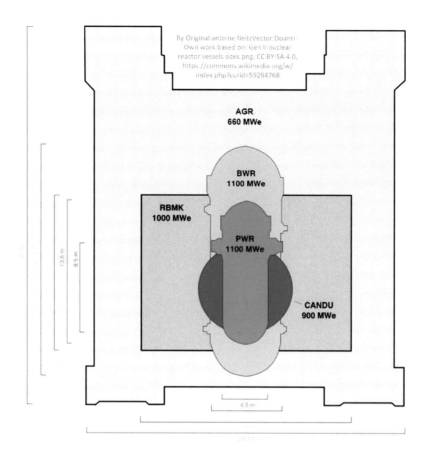

AGR
660 MWe

BWR
1100 MWe

RBMK
1000 MWe

PWR
1100 MWe

CANDU
900 MWe

Figure 4 Comparison of reactor sizes

As well as moderation, the graphite provides structural integrity and a large heat capacity to absorb the heat from small variations in power levels.

Given the size of the core and the space required above the core for the fuelling machine to take used fuel out and add fresh fuel, it is not practical to include a sealed containment building around the structure. This is a lower level of protection than that found on most reactors.

The graphite is contained in the reactor cavity formed from a cylindrical steel construction and a top and bottom structure. The top of the reactor is a concrete lid.

Heat is generated by nuclear fission within the fuel and by the interaction of the gamma rays and neutrons produced by fission and fission fragment decay in the material of the reactor. Notably the graphite moderator gets very hot in some places.

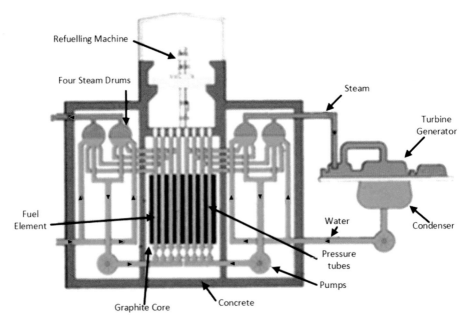

Refuelling Machine

Four Steam Drums

Steam

Turbine Generator

Fuel Element

Water

Condenser

Pressure tubes

Pumps

Graphite Core

Concrete

From https://nucleus.iaea.org/sites/graphiteknowledgebase/wiki/Guide_to_Graphite/Other%20Designs%20of%20Nuclear%20Power%20Stations.aspx

Figure 5 RBMK Reactor layout

The graphite has a maximum permitted temperature of 730°C compared water at the core inlet of 265-270°C and outlet at 284°C (Ref. 20). Graphite heat is 5.5% of core thermal power (Ref. 21). A mixture of nitrogen and helium is circulated between the graphite blocks to prevent oxidation of the graphite and to cool the graphite.

Heat is removed from the reactor by pumping water in at the bottom and passing it up the insides of individual pressure tubes. Someway up the reactor the water boils and changes to a water/steam mixture. Exactly where this happens depends on a number of factors including the degree of *sub-cooling* of the water entering the reactor (i.e. how far below the boiling point for that pressure it is), the rate of pumping and the power level of the reactor. **This is important to the accident sequence.** The stream is withdrawn from the top of the reactor, separated from the water droplets and used to turn steam turbines which turn a generator which produces electricity. The steam is condensed (turned back to water), pumped into the water section of the steam separators and pumped back into the bottom of the reactor.

The reactor has two cooling loops each with a 500 MWe turbine. The reactor produces 3200 MWt[7].

---

[7] A note on reactor power: Nuclear reactors use the fission reaction to produce heat. This heat is used to produce steam which drives turbines which turn a generator to produce electricity.

The graphite is used to slow down or *moderate* the neutrons. This is done because neutrons produced by fission have a high energy (average about 2 MeV)[8] and are therefore moving fast. Fission is much more likely with slow neutrons, or *thermal neutrons*, hence the need to slow fission-neutrons. Thermal neutrons are so called because they have a similar kinetic energy to the atoms or molecules around them and so are at the same temperature. Thermal neutrons have a range of energies clustered around[9] 0.04 eV. See section B.5 for more detail.

Control rods, some under automatic control and some under manual control, are used to control the total power output of the reactor and the relative power of different sectors of the reactor. These consist of a material that absorbs neutrons extremely well that can be inserted or withdrawn as required. A reactor safety feature is that the control systems limit the number of rods that can be pulled out at the same time and limit the speed with which rods can be withdrawn. This is to limit the rate at which reactor power can be raised. Conversely all reactors have a *scram*[10] mechanism that drops all available rods into the reactor as fast as possible to quench the chain reaction. See section 5.1 for more detail.

RBMK reactors were used mainly for *base load* which means that they operated at the same power output for a long time while other generating plants, such as coal

---

There are energy losses within this chain so the reactor produces more kilowatts of heat energy than the kilowatts of electricity produced by the generator. Two values are therefore presented: the thermal output of the reactor MW(t) (mega-watt thermal), which is the heat generated in the reactor, and the electrical output of the generator MW(e) (mega-watt electrical), which is the electricity produced. The latter is the smaller. Efforts are made to make reactors thermally efficient to increase the electrical output without using more nuclear fuel. The RBMK design of reactor has a "thermal efficiency" of about 33% [(2 x 500MW)/3200MW].

[8] In reactor physics energies are often measured in electron-volts (eV), the energy an electron gains falling through an electric potential difference of one volt. This is very small (1 eV = 1.602 x 10^{-19} Joules) so SI multipliers k (kilo) = 1,000 and M (mega) = 1,000,000 are often used.

[9] The energy distribution of neutrons in thermal equilibrium with the medium they are in would be given by the Maxwell-Boltzmann distribution. The most probable energy is given by E = kT where k is the Boltzmann constant (k = $8.52 \cdot 10^{-5}$ eV/K) and T is the temperature in kelvin. At a reactor temperature of 320°C (593 K), a value characteristic for PWRs, the most probable velocity is 3100 m/s and the corresponding energy is 0.051 eV.

You can check the relationship between velocity and energy using the equation E = ½m.v^2 with m (the mass of the neutron) = 1.675 x 10^{-27} kg, energy in J, mass in kg and velocity in m.s^{-1} and remembering that 1 eV = 1.602 x 10^{-19} J.

[10] Reactor folk law tells us that the term SCRAM stands for Safety Control Rod Axe Man and relates to the emergency shutdown system on the Chicago Pile No 1 (the first critical assembly). This consisted of control rods suspended by ropes at the top of the pile. An axe was available to cut the rope and send the rods in to quench the chain reaction. As criticality was approached a man stood by, axe in hand, ready to react at the first sign of trouble. He was the prototype scram system. Sadly the Nuclear Regulatory Commission historian tells us that this explanation may not be true (Ref. 22).

powered stations, were turned up and down to match the changes in electrical demands on the network.

A very comprehensive and clear description of the Smolensk-3 Nuclear Power Plant, a more modern RBMK, is given by Parisi (Ref. 23). Table 1 gives some of the key properties of the Chernobyl RBMK.

Boiling water reactors are quite common. The UK Steam Generating Heavy Water Reactor, of which only a prototype was built, is one example. A description of this reactor, designed as back-up in case the AGR ran into problems, can be found in Ref. 24. A short description of modern Boiling Water Reactors can be found in Ref. 25.

Ref. 26 reports an overview of a British view of the RBMK reactor design flaws, by Lord Walter Marshall, who was chairman of the Central Electricity Generating Board. This view was based on the UK investigation of a similar design and, it is claimed, communicated to the Soviets before the accident.

The flaws listed include:

- The positive void coefficient;
- Variations in neutron flux across the reactor;
- The graphite is very hot;
- Weak structure and lack of containment;
- Lack of diverse core cooling;
- Complex piping "a plumber's nightmare".

The important things to take from this section is that the RBMK is a large reactor, moderated by graphite blocks, cooled by a water and steam mixture and consists of a large number of individual pressure tubes containing fuel and water. Control is by a number of sets of control rods, some of which are under automatic control and some under manual control.

3. Outline of the accident

3.1. Introduction

This section is a summary of the events leading up to the accident. It includes many technical terms which are explained later in the text. A fuller description is given in Section 6 after the background physics have been introduced.

A lot has been written about the Chernobyl accident. Some of this is very detailed and some is more general. Some is inaccurate and misleading. Some is still speculation as there are elements of the story upon which the investigators disagree (see, for example, Ref. 27). I have based my descriptions on a relatively short article

Characteristic	Value
Thermal Power (MW)	3200
Fuel Enrichment (%)	2.0
Mass of Uranium in fuel assembly (kg)	114.7
Number/diameter of fuel rods in fuel assembly (mm)	18/13.6
Fuel burn-up (MW.d/kg)	20
Axial power peaking factor	1.40
Radial power peaking factor	1.48
Maximum design power of fuel channel (kW)	3000
Void coefficient of reactivity at working point ($\%^{-1}$ ($\partial k/k$) void)	$+2.0 \times 10^{-4}$
Fast power coefficient of reactivity at the working point (MW^{-1})	-0.5×10^{-6}
Fuel temperature coefficient of reactivity ($^{\circ}C^{-1}$)	-1.2×10^{-5}
Graphite temperature coefficient of reactivity	6×10^{-5}
Maximum efficiency of RCPS rods (%)	10.5
Efficiency of manual control rods (%)	7.5
Effect (on average) of replacing a spent fuel assembly (%)	0.02

Table 1 Characteristics of RBMK (INSAG-7)

by the World Nuclear Association (whose technical descriptions I tend to trust) (Ref. 28), on information provided by the Soviets for an IAEA meeting (Ref. 29), on the International Atomic Energy Agency's second very detailed report INSAG-7 (Ref. 13), on two articles by the plant's former deputy chief engineer, A Dyatlov (who drew up the experiment plan and was in the control room on the fateful night), responding to some criticism of the Chernobyl crew (Refs. 30 and 31), on an article written by Mikhail V. Malko of the National Academy of Sciences of Belarus (Ref. 32), on a seminar paper written by F. Motte (Ref. 33), and some well researched, if not entirely impartial, books written by knowledgeable people (Ref. 34 - Ref. 38). Reading these you get the very clear impression that the first IAEA report (INSAG-1) (Ref. 39), based largely on a conference discussing the first Soviet report, was overly ready to blame the team on duty at the time of the accident rather than to look for deeper root causes. I have been unable to get a copy of this report either on the internet or from the IAEA, which I think is telling.

3.2. The Experiment

If the pumps pushing the coolant water around the primary circuit slow or stop for any reason then the amount of cooling will be reduced. If the cooling is less than the heat being produced then the reactor will get hotter and can be damaged if temperature limits are exceeded. These pumps are therefore very important, particularly in reactors with a high power density. The RBMK uses electrically powered pumps. In normal operation the electricity to power the pumps comes from the site power supplies which include the output from the reactor, output from neighbouring reactors or electricity taken from the national power grid. The design of the Chernobyl site included emergency back-up diesel generators to make the electricity required to keep these pumps working if all the site power supplies failed but these needed some time to start up (about 45 seconds).

The important question being asked was "in the event of a sudden site power supply failure, can we use the slowing down turbines to provide enough electricity to keep the reactor cooling pumps and feed-water pumps operating sufficiently well to prevent reactor damage until the emergency diesels can take over?

The concept of the experiment was simple. At the end of a power run, when the reactor was going to be shut down for routine maintenance anyway, they were going to disconnect the steam supply to one of the turbines and let it run down while connected to the generator to see how much power they could harvest before the turbine slowed too much. It is important to understand that this was seen as, and indeed was, an electrical experiment on peripheral equipment and not a reactor experiment. The role of the reactor was to get the turbine spinning at full speed so that the experiment could start, after which the reactor could be shutdown.

In line with the experiment design the reactor power was slowly reduced to 50% in a controlled manner (only one of the two turbines was being used in the experiment). One of the turbines (No. 7)[11] was disconnected at 13:05:00. The power for auxiliary equipment (4 main cooling pumps, 2 electrical feed water pumps, etc.) were transferred to turbine No. 8. This was the equipment involved in the test. Two other main cooling pumps were powered from the grid with two more connected to the grid but on standby i.e. not being used but ready to go at the flick of a switch if needed.

Shortly before the experiment was due the site was ordered to delay disconnection from the grid to meet demand for electricity. One of the consequences of this was that the shift that had prepared for the test was not going to be there. Instead a less prepared, and less experienced shift was going to be manning the reactor control

---

[11] Turbines 1-6 would have been on reactors 1 - 3.

room during the test.

Nine hours later the work on the experiment restarted and the reactor power reduction was resumed. During the power reduction an automatic control system was initiated which erroneously reduced the power to near zero. This initiated a xenon transient[12] which hampered attempts to recover the reactor power to the level called for in the experiment design, a power level at which it could provide enough steam to spin the turbine fast enough to start the experiment. This was an opportunity to reconsider if the conditions were right to proceed with the test. It was an opportunity spurned and the operators, under instruction bordering on bullying, struggled to recover reactor power levels. Chernobyl's place in history may have been very different if they had taken a more cautious approach to nuclear safety[13]. The operators got the reactor back to 200 MW$_t$, still below the target reactor power for the experiment.

Changing the power output of a nuclear reactor causes a number of changes in temperatures and pressures around the system and that requires a number of pumps and valves to be put on different settings. It also initiates changes in the concentrations of some fission fragments within the nuclear fuel. These changes in temperatures, flow rates, pressures and fission fragments can all affect the number of neutrons available to initiate fissions and they can all affect each other in a variety of ways as explained throughout the remainder of this book[14].

The most significant occurrences that night were an ingrowth of Xenon-135 following the unplanned changes in reactor power; a reduction in steam quality caused by pumping excessive volumes of water, reducing the voidage in the cooling circuit; and a cooling of the reactor graphite. All of these effects increased the wastage of neutrons causing control rods to move out of the reactor to compensate. When the operators tried to increase the power to the levels required for the experiment they moved the rods even further out, beyond the permitted operating

---

[12] This is the temporary build-up of neutron absorbing fission products in the cooling circuit which follows a power drop and can make it difficult to restart a reactor. It is explained later, see section 4.3.5.

[13] Although some accounts state that this "was an accident waiting to happen". If it had been avoided that day the chances were it would happen on a later date, maybe at a different RBMK.

[14] A significant part of the training for a reactor operator consists of questions along the line of "what would happen to reactor power if we opened a particular valve while at 80% power?" The answer usually has several layers as the effects ripple through the fuel temperature, cooling circuit temperature and pressure, reactor internal temperature and the neutron economy (reactivity). The change in temperature of the fuel is rapid while the change in temperature of the reactor structure and moderator is slower. With complex effects of differing signs and differing time scales it can be challenging to give a comprehensive answer under classroom conditions. In reactor control rooms, on the other hand, most changes in power levels are slow and controllable and automatic systems do most of the work.

range. Why this mattered was more subtle than some would have you believe. If the operators had known they were outside the operational limits and understood the gravity of the situation they may have been able to save the reactor but their instrument panels were not showing any particularly worrying abnormalities before the experiment started. One relatively obscure output was showing the breach of operational limits on the number of control rods removed from the reactor but this was not seen as a safety indicator.

Motte (Ref. 33) reports that *"to bring the reactor back to 200 MWth (which was as a high as they could get it), the operator had pulled far too many of the manual control rods out of the reactor.*

According to the rules, the operation reactivity margin[15] is not allowed to go below 30 rod equivalents without special authorization of the chief engineer of the plant. If this margin falls below 15 rod equivalents, nobody can authorize continued operation of the plant.

The operation reactivity margin, with the reactor power back to 200 MWth, had dropped to between six and eight rod equivalents".

Pulling so many rods so far out brought into play two design faults of the safety rods[16] and a design fault of the reactor[17]

At the same time the configuration of the cooling circuits moved to a position where they were unstable. The operators took the unusual step of having all eight main coolant pumps running at the same time (usually two, one on each side, are held in reserve). This was so that they could keep the reactor at power in case they needed to run up the turbine for another attempt of the experiment. This resulted in coolant flow rates in excess of the normal rates while the reactor was operating at a low power output[18]. As a result, the void fraction (amount of steam) was low. With poor steam quality a larger fraction than usual of the coolant was being recycled from the steam separators without going through the turbines and the temperature difference between the coolant at the top of the reactor and the bottom of the reactor narrowed. At this stage the water at the reactor inlet was near its boiling point (3° of sub-cooling). Small increases in temperatures or small drops in pressure would lead to a significant increase in boiling within the reactor fuel channels with important

---

[15] A measure of the number of control rods inserted into the reactor. See Section 5.4.

[16] Their slow insertion speed, as they had to push through a narrow pipe and displace cooling water, and their graphite displacers hung below them which added, rather than removed, reactivity on initial insertion from fully out.

[17] Its positive void coefficient.

[18] The experiment design called for all the pumps to be on at this stage but the experiment was designed for a higher power level at which the cooling system would have been more stable.

consequences for the neutron economy.

On the initiation of the experiment several design flaws came into play.

To start the experiment, the turbine stream lines were closed as planned. The disconnection of the turbine caused the coolant water temperature to rise (because the turbines had stopped removing energy) and, since the water was near to its boiling point, induced boiling. It is thought that the boiling might have been lower in the reactor than was normal because of the small value of sub-cooling (water was entering the bottom of the reactor at near boiling point). This produced a sharp increase in voidage (steam bubbles in the water), adding reactivity. The control rods were released shortly afterwards. Because of the bad design and unusual location of the control rods they initially added even more reactivity to the lower half of the reactor, increasing the rate of fission. As they moved painfully slowly this phase lasted for longer than should have been necessary. This resulted in more local reactivity, resulting in more heating in the bottom half of the reactor which changed more of the cooling water to steam lower down the pressure tubes. The reactor's "positive void coefficient", another major design flaw, came into play here. As water turned to steam, fewer neutrons were absorbed in the water and so more remained available to cause more fissions adding further heating and forming more steam. This is a "positive feedback" situation; rises in temperature causing a change that leads to further rises in temperature. This is not an easy situation to control[19].

The reactor power surged to an estimated 100 times full power in less than a minute. This would not have been uniform across the large core and some sections would have become extremely hot very quickly.

Pressure tubes failed under the power surge leading to a drop in pressure, more steam (less water) and more neutrons. The hot water hit hot graphite and flashed into steam. The top of the reactor was blown away by the initial pressure surge which was followed by another massive explosion which was possibly caused by the burning of hydrogen that had been generated by the contact of overheated fuel and water.

With the reactor containment lost, reactor components scattered around the site and fires burning within the reactor and on roofs, the worst nuclear accident to date had happened.

---

[19] By contrast, in a PWR which is cooled and moderated by liquid water and is designed to be under moderated, an increase in temperature leads to an expansion of the water reducing its ability to moderate. Removing moderator from an under moderated reactor reduces the reactivity so the reactor slows down. It is self-correcting.

4. Sufficient nuclear and reactor physics

The reactors at Chernobyl, like all nuclear reactors, utilised the nuclear fission chain reaction to produce heat. To understand the accident at Chernobyl you need to understand a little about the chain reaction. Two aspects are particularly important; the neutron economy and delayed neutrons.

This section looks at the role of neutrons in a nuclear reactor and their role in the Chernobyl accident.

The atom, and particularly the nucleus, are nothing like the world we experience; distances are very small, mass and energy densities are very high, time scales are very short, forces can be extremely strong. The classical physics of Newton et al fails under these conditions and quantum effects dominate. This makes explanation and understanding more difficult and means that many features of nuclear physics will be described rather than truly explained.

4.1. The atomic nucleus

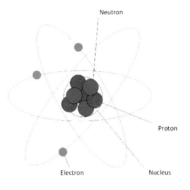

We now understand that matter is composed of *atoms* which consists of *neutrons* and *protons* tightly bound to each other in the centre of the atom, its *nucleus.*

Electrons "orbit" the nucleus in a series of shells at a relatively large distance.

- The radius of an atom is about 0.1 nm to 0.5 nm (1 × 10^{-10} m - 5 × 10^{-10}m).[20]
- The radius of a nucleus is about (1 × 10^{-14} m) is less than 1/10,000 of the radius of an atom.[21]
- Nuclei are extremely dense, averaging 1.8 × 10^{14} grams per cubic centimetre compared to water's density of 1 gram per cubic centimetre.

Figure 6 The atom

It is not necessary to understand anything about the structure of the neutron, proton or electron to understand reactor physics provided you are willing to take "on-trust" some rather strange outcomes such as beta decay.

---

[20] Since neither the atom nor the nucleus has a clearly defined outer boundary care should be taken when interpreting statements about the size of either.

[21] Notwithstanding the previous footnote, the radius of the nucleus can be reasonably well fitted using the equation r = (1.25 x 10^{-15} m) $A^{1/3}$ where: r = radius of the nucleus (m) and A = atomic mass number (dimensionless)

In a number of circumstances neutrons and protons (collectively called nucleons) can be treated as featureless entities with the properties given in Table 2.

	Relative mass	Relative charge
Proton	1	+1
Neutron	1	0
Electron	1/1840	-1

Table 2 Relative mass and charge of main sub-atomic particles

The number of protons in the nucleus (referred to as the atomic number and by the letter Z) determines the chemical identity of the atom. The number of protons plus neutrons determines the **mass number** (referred to by the letter A) of the atom. The number of neutrons is generally denoted by the letter N.

There are various ways in which nuclides can be written. For tritium, which is hydrogen-3 (1 proton and 2 neutrons) these include:

^{3}H $^{3}_{1}H$ H-3   t   3-hydrogen   hydrogen-3

In the neutral atom the number of protons in the nucleus is equalled by the number of electrons "orbiting" the nucleus.

In this model of the atom, hydrogen, for example, is pictured as a negatively charged electron orbiting a positively charged proton. This picture is adequate for an understanding of the Chernobyl accident. For a more modern description of the atom see Section A.1.

Within the nucleus it is found that some combinations of numbers of neutrons and protons are stable, meaning that these nuclei will last pretty much forever unless involved in a violent nuclear collision. Others, with less acceptable combinations of neutrons and protons, will rearrange themselves unto more stable configurations spitting out unwanted sub-atomic particles and energy as they do so. This process is called *radioactive decay*. A number of different nuclear models are used to explain why some combinations of neutron and protons are stable, why some can exist for a period of time but tend to break up naturally (unstable or radioactive isotopes) and why some are never formed.

Most elements (each Z number) have stable forms with different numbers of neutrons. These are called "*isotopes*". For example Hydrogen, with 1 proton (Z=1) has 3 naturally occurring isotopes. It can exist with 2 neutrons (A=3), 1 neutron (A=2) or no neutrons (A=1).

These can be written:

^3_1H $\qquad\qquad$ ^2_1H $\qquad\qquad$ and $\qquad$ ^1_1H

The heavier isotopes of hydrogen are also known as deuterium (hydrogen-2) and tritium (hydrogen-3). The hydrogen found on earth is 99.9885% H-1, 0.0115% H-2 with a trace of H-3.

Note: references such as Ref. 40 list properties for even more neutron rich isotopes of hydrogen, going out to H-7. These do not appear in nature, having half-lives measured in yocto-seconds (10^{-24} s – I had to look that one up!). Research on these exotic nuclei allows nuclear models, and therefore our understanding of the nuclear world, to be tested in extreme circumstances.

A great deal of data about which combinations of nucleons are stable and which are unstable can be found on the internet, often summarised in the form of Segre charts (see Section A.2 and Ref. 41).

All you really need to take from this section is that matter is made of atoms and atoms are made of neutrons and protons in a central massive nucleus with electrons "orbiting" at a comparatively large distance.

4.2. Fission chain reaction

In this section we meet the fission process and chain reaction that power nuclear reactors.

The nuclei that we discussed in the previous section can be broken apart and reassembled in different configurations. Radioactivity is one result of this. Radioactivity is where an unstable nucleus reorganises itself, spitting out unwanted particles and energy. Very large nuclei can also *fission,* that is break into two or more fragments giving out energy in the process.

Nuclear reactors utilize the fission of heavy nuclei, usually an isotope of uranium, namely U-235, to generate heat which is used to make steam to drive turbines and thus to generate electricity.

In the chain reaction (Figure 7) a thermal (slow moving) neutron is absorbed into the nucleus of a U-235 atom. The U-235 nucleus contains 92 protons and 143 neutrons. Adding another neutron makes the nucleus into unstable excited U-236. Most (about 85.5%[22]) of the U-236 nuclei undergo a process called "fission". That is, they split into two (usually[23]) large fission fragments and a number of fast (highly energetic)

---

[22] The remainder emits the excess energy as gamma radiation and remains as U-236.
[23] In less than 0.5% of fissions a third small charged fission fragment is formed in a process called "*ternary fission*" as opposed to the more likely "*binary fission*".

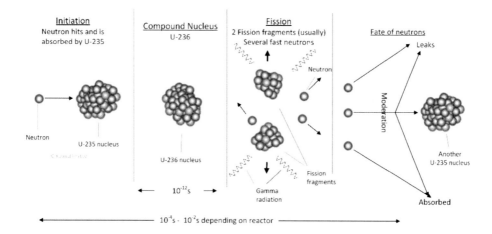

Figure 7 The chain reaction

neutrons (average about 2.45 for thermal fission of U-235, see Table 3). This takes about 10^{-14} seconds and liberates energy.

About 85% of the energy produced in fission is the kinetic energy of the fission fragments which is converted to heat within the fuel as they stop within microscopic distances. Some energy is converted to gamma rays emitted at the moment of fission and some is converted to the kinetic energy of the neutrons. Additional energy and neutrons are liberated by the radioactive decay of fission fragments. More detail is given in Table 3 and Table 4.

N° of neutrons	0	1	2	3	4	5
Probability (%)	2	17	36	31	12	3

Table 3 Probability distribution of number of neutrons emitted, thermal fission of U-235

There are a large number of possible fission reactions (JEF- 3.3, a database of nuclear reactions, lists 873 isotopes with non-zero independent fission fragment yields for thermal fission of U-235).

For example

$$U\text{-}235 + n \longrightarrow Ba\text{-}144 + Kr\text{-}90 + 2n$$
$$U\text{-}235 + n \longrightarrow Ba\text{-}141 + Kr\text{-}92 + 3n$$
$$U\text{-}235 + n \longrightarrow Zr\text{-}94 + Te\text{-}139 + 3n$$

Fission yields will be discussed in more detail later (Section B.2).

Mode of appearance		MeV	%	Notes
Directly from fission	Kinetic energy of fission fragments	166.2	82.4	Deposited within a few tens of microns in the fuel matrix. (Heats fuel).
	Prompt gamma rays	8	4.2	High energy gamma rays emitted at the point of fission.
	Kinetic energy of neutrons from fission	4.8	2.4	Mainly deposited in the moderator.
Radioactive decay of fission fragments	Gamma	7.2	3.6	Decay heat and radioactivity of used fuel.
	Beta	7	3.5	
	Neutrino	(9.6)	0	Energy lost from system
From neutron capture gammas	(n,γ) reactions	8.4	4.2	Average binding energy of neutron (6 MeV) x number of neutrons captured on average (1.4).
Total without neutrinos		201.6		

Table 4 Energy from Fission – From Ref. 42

The important message from this section has been that fission is a process in which a large nucleus breaks up producing energy, neutrons and fission fragments. Importantly there are isotopes, such as U-235, that can be induced to fission by hitting them with a neutron. A chain reaction can then be envisaged in which neutrons produced in fission go on to induce more fissions and this cycle, or chain reaction, can repeat indefinitely.

4.3. Neutron economy

This is essentially an accounting process to understand the different fates that may await a neutron produced in a fission reaction. It is important to understand this concept so that we can understand nuclear reactor control. It is less important to understand the mathematical formulation but it is not at all hard.

4.3.1.   Effective multiplication factor

Different fates can await the fast neutrons produced in fission; they can fly out of the reactor, they can be absorbed in the reactor internals, they can be slowed down (moderated or thermalized) by interaction with the materials they pass through, and they can go on to induce another fission (more likely after slowing down than before).

If on average one neutron from each fission goes on to induce another then the rate of reaction will be constant and we say that the reactor is *critical*. If the average is less than one then the power is reducing and the reactor is sub-critical.

To gain insight into this cycle we introduce the *effective multiplication factor k* (sometimes shown as k_{eff} to distinguish it from k_∞ the *infinite multiplication factor* which applies to infinite sized assembles).

The effective multiplication factor can be expressed as:

$$k = \frac{\text{Number of neutrons in a generation}}{\text{Number of neutron in the previous generation}}$$

k is a dimensionless number.

k is a measure of the fractional change in the number of neutrons in the reactor over an, as yet unspecified, period of time equivalent to one cycle or "link" of the chain.

If k is greater than one then the number of neutrons and the power generated by the reactor core is increasing with time. If k is less than one then the reaction is dying away with time (See Figure 8).

The art of running a nuclear reactor is to be able to control k so that power can be raised safety (k > 1 but not too high), kept at constant power (k = 1) and shut down (k <1) when desired.

We are now going to embark on an accounting exercise to consider, and quantify, the possible fates of neutrons produced in fission. This is key to understanding reactor control (or in the case of Chernobyl, loss of control).

Consider a cycle starting with n thermal neutrons being absorbed in fuel (U-235 nuclei) and inducing fission reactions. If the average number of neutrons produced by these fission reactions is η per fission (the Greek letter eta, η, is generally used for this value) then the process produces $n\eta$ fission neutrons (n fissions multiplied by η fission neutrons per fission). These neutrons would each have a lot of kinetic energy (they would be fast neutrons).

From n fissions you get, on average, $n\eta$ fission neutrons (where we have introduced the "reproduction factor" η)

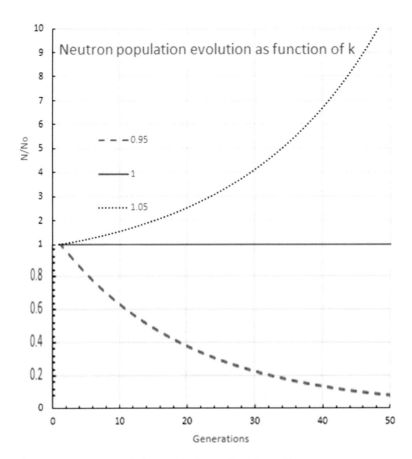

Figure 8 neutron population evolution as function of k

Some of these fission neutrons may induce fission in 235-U or 238-U atoms before they have been appreciably slowed down. This will increase the number of fast neutrons in the system. This can be accounted for by including a *fast fission factor, ϵ* (this is the Greek letter epsilon, ϵ). The number of fast neutrons is now $n\eta\epsilon$ from the original n absorbed thermal neutrons.

After taking account of extra neutrons produced by the fission induced by fast neutrons there are $n\eta\epsilon$ fast neutrons following from n fissions. (Introduction of fast fission factor).

In a finite system some of the fast neutrons may escape from the reactor volume. Those remaining are given by $n\eta\epsilon P_{FNL}$ where the fast non-leakage probability, P_{FNL}, has been introduced.

After taking account of the neutrons that stream out of the reactor as fast neutrons there are $n\eta\epsilon P_{FNL}$ remaining neutrons. (Introduction of fast non-leakage factor).

The remaining neutrons undergo a series of interactions with the materials around them getting progressively slower as they do. During this process they can be absorbed in materials other than fissile nuclei and are lost to the system. As they slow down the neutrons' kinetic energy reduces. At some energies absorption is very much more likely than others, a process called *resonance absorption*. We assign ρ (Greek letter rho, ρ) as the resonance escape probability which is the fraction that become thermalized rather than absorbed on the way. The number of thermal neutrons in the system is then $n\,\eta\,\epsilon\,P_{FNL}\,\rho$.

The number of slow neutrons produced by n fissions can be presented by $n\eta\epsilon\rho P_{FNL}$. (Introduction of resonance escape factor).

Some of the slow neutrons will escape from the reactor. We assign P_{TNL} as the thermal non-leakage factor.

After taking account of the neutrons that stream out of the reactor as slow neutrons there are $n\eta\epsilon\rho P_{FNL}P_{TNL}$ remaining neutrons. (Introduction of thermal non-leakage factor).

Of these thermal neutrons a fraction f (*thermal utilisation factor*) will be absorbed in fuel and initiate further fissions. The cycle is complete.

The number of second generation fissions resulting from n first generation fissions is given by the product of (multiplying them together) $\eta f \rho \epsilon\ P_{FNL}\ P_{TNL}$. (Introduction of thermal utilisation factor).

This can be summarised in the six-factor equation $\quad k\ =\ \eta.\,f.\,\rho.\,\epsilon.\,P_{FNL}.\,P_{TNL}$

which is an extension of Fermi's four-factor formula $\ k_\infty\ =\ \eta.\,f.\,\rho.\,\epsilon \qquad$ (Ref. 46)

with

k_∞ = Multiplication factor $\left(\dfrac{\text{Number of neutrons in a generation}}{\text{Number of neutrons in preceeding generation}}\right)$ for an
infinite core.

$\eta\ $ = Reproduction factor = $\left(\dfrac{\text{Neutrons produced by fuel}}{\text{Neutrons absorbed by fuel}}\right)$

$f\ $ = Thermal utilisation factor = $\left(\dfrac{\text{neutrons absorbed by the fuel}}{\text{neutrons absorbed in total}}\right)$

$\rho\ $ = The resonance escape probability = $\left(\dfrac{\text{Fission neutrons that become thermalised}}{\text{total number of fission neutrons produced}}\right)$

$\epsilon\ $ = The fast fission factor = $\left(\dfrac{\text{total number of fission neutrons produced}}{\text{number of fission neutrons from thermal fission}}\right)$

Now generalising to a finite core

$$k\ =\ \eta.\,f.\,\rho.\,\epsilon.\,P_{FNL}.\,P_{TNL}$$

P_{FNL} = Fast non-leakage probability (The probability that a fast neutron will NOT leak)

P_{TNL} = Thermal non-leakage probability (the probability that a thermal neutron will NOT leak).

Putting some slightly arbitrary numbers in this equation to help understand it. See Table 5 which considers a critical reactor with 1000 neutrons in each generation (this is a very low power reactor!).

All of these terms can be affected by the design and operation of the reactor.

Leakage can be reduced by making the reactor bigger, making the material of the reactor better at intercepting neutrons, or by adding an outer layer of material with a low-Z component (that is, contains light nuclei such as hydrogen and carbon) to reflect some of the straying neutrons back into the core (hence the "reflector" you may notice in a number of reactor designs).

Resonance escape can be enhanced by reducing the prevalence of materials that absorb neutrons as they are slowing down, hence the materials used in reactors are carefully chosen and minimum use of materials is made. This term is also sensitive to temperature. This is because a rise in temperature results in greater movement of the atoms in the fuel matrix. This makes it more likely that there will be an exact energy match between the sum of the kinetic and binding energies of the neutron and the excited state of the resulting nucleus making absorption far more probable as the system does not need to cope with a mismatch of energy.

Resonance escape is also enhanced by using heterogeneous reactors. In these the nuclear fuel is in the form of rods or plates surrounded by just the right thickness of moderator. A fast neutron heading out from a fuel pin passes through fuel-less moderator where it loses energy without fear of resonance capture and then enters a fuel rod or plate as a thermalized neutron, below the resonance absorption energies and ready to induce fission. Unenriched U-235 cannot be made to sustain a chain reaction without this trick.

Thermal utilisation can also be enhanced by reducing the amount of neutron absorbing material within the core or by increasing the number of fissile nuclei by *enriching* the fuel (increasing the proportion of U-235).

A quite detailed and readable description of how these factors change over time and during power changes for a PWR can be found in Ref. 47.

Stage	Factor	Cumulative	Number of neutrons remaining	Number lost in this stage
Fast fission	ϵ, The fast fission factor (1.03)	ϵ	1030	30 extra neutrons produced by fast fissions
Fast non-leakage	P_{FNL}, Fast non-leakage probability (0.95)	$\epsilon.P_{FNL}$	979	51 fast neutrons lost to leakage
Resonance escape	ρ, The resonance escape probability (0.75)	$\rho.\epsilon.P_{FNL}$	734	245 neutrons absorbed during moderation
Thermal non-leakage	P_{TNL}, Thermal non-leakage probability (0.96)	$\rho.\epsilon.P_{FNL}.P_{TNL}$	705	29 neutrons lost to leakage as thermal neutrons
Thermal utilisation	f, Thermal utilisation factor (0.70)	$f.\rho.\epsilon.P_{FNL}.P_{TNL}$	494 thermal induced fissions	211 thermal neutrons absorbed in non-fuel materials
Fast neutrons produced by fissions	η, Reproduction factor (2.02)	$\eta.f.\rho.\epsilon.P_{FNL}.P_{TNL}$	1000 thermal neutrons produced	

Table 5 - Fission chain reactor: possible fates of neutrons with indicative numbers

The assessment of the possible changes in reactivity in normal and accident conditions is an important and complex part of the safety assessment of nuclear reactors.

The important thing to take from this section is that we can gain an instructive understanding of the neutron economy by considering what could happen to a neutron emitted during a fission. However, as we will see later, the parameterisation (putting real values for $\eta.f.\rho.\epsilon.P_{FNL}.P_{TNL}$ into the six factor equation) is more complex as there are a number of factors and interrelationships to take into account for each of them.

In a critical reactor, there is a balance between the neutron production (through fission), absorption (in the fuel, moderator and the reactor materials) and leakage (out through the reactor boundaries).

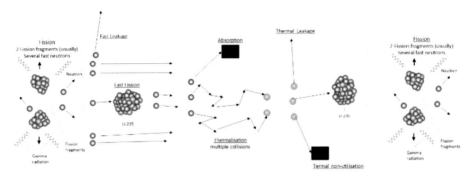

Figure 9 Variety of possible neutron fates

4.3.2. Reactivity

In Section 4.3.1 we derived an expression for the ratio of neutrons in the system in successive generations which we called k_{eff}. While this gives useful insight, it is not the best term for reactor analysis.

A more useful term for the mathematicians is found to be the deviation from an effective multiplication factor of one. We introduce the term *reactivity* (usually denoted by either ρ or Δk/k).

$$\rho = \frac{k_{eff} - 1}{k_{eff}}$$

A critical reactor (one at stable power) has ρ = 0 while a super-critical reactor (power density growing exponentially) has ρ > 0.

ρ is a dimensionless number.

Reactivity is just another way of showing that a reactor is sub-critical, critical or super-critical. It is used in reactor physics because it simplifies the form of some of the equations involved in reactor analysis.

4.3.3. Coefficients of reactivity

This section looks at those factors that affect a reactor's reactivity (criticality) during operation. Coefficients of reactivity are a measure of how much the reactivity changes in response to a unit change of one of the parameters to which it is sensitive.

4.3.3.1. Principles

Coefficients of reactivity provide a measure of how the reactivity (neutron multiplication) of a reactor core varies as a function of other variables such as temperature and pressure and are important for understanding the stability, or instability, of reactors undergoing changes. The five main parameters that can affect reactivity during normal and accident conditions are the coolant density, the graphite temperature, the coolant temperature, the fuel density and the fuel temperature. In an RBMK fuel density and coolant temperature are of minor importance compared to the other three.

Changing the amount of moderator in a reactor will change the energy distribution of the neutrons which will affect all the phenomena with energy-dependent cross-sections, most particularly resonance absorption and thermal utilisation. Adding more moderator to an under-moderated system will reduce the fast leakage and resonance absorption (i.e. increase resonance escape) and therefore increase the thermal utilisation. This will increase the reactivity of the system. However, in an over moderated system, adding more moderator increases absorption in the moderator (reducing the thermal utilisation) without improving the moderation, so thermal utilisation is reduced. Figure 10 summarises the effect of changing the moderator to fuel ratio in a large reactor. It shows that there is an optimum ratio above which the reactor is "over moderated" and below which it is "under moderated". The moderator coefficient of reactivity can therefore be of either positive or negative depending on the reactor design[24]. In the RBMK, moderation is performed in the graphite, thus changes in the temperature or density of the cooling water do not significantly affect moderation.

Adding more materials that absorb thermal neutrons without resulting in a fission will result in more neutrons being wasted and the thermal utilisation factor being reduced. This is how control rods, burnable poisons and low voidage fractions in coolant water reduce reactivity.

Many fission fragments will absorb neutrons and their build-up during operation must be taken into account[25]. Xe-135 is important in this respect because it has an unusually high neutron absorption cross section. It played an important role in the Chernobyl accident.

---

[24] Operating PWRs, which use the same water both as coolant and moderator, are generally designed to operate as under-moderated. If any change causes the PWR power density to rise, the water temperature will increase, its density will decrease and it will become a poorer moderator which will tend to reduce the power of the reactor. This "negative coefficient of power" is important for the reactor's operational safety.

[25] Early operating experience with the first nuclear reactor, Chicago or Fermi Pile No 1, showed that the reactor slowly lost reactivity after achieving criticality and poisoning by fission products was suspected (See Ref. 49) for a first-hand account of this period.

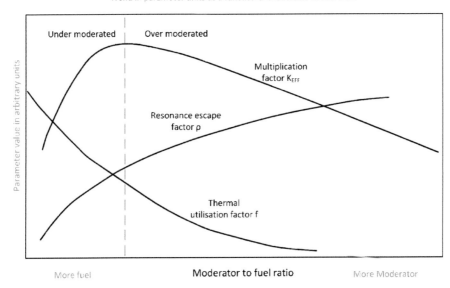

Figure 10 moderator to fuel ratio impact on multiplication factor

Fuel temperature plays an important role in reactivity. As temperature increases the thermal motion of the atoms within the fuel matrix increases. This increases the width of the neutron absorption resonances which significantly increases resonance absorption[26]. The fuel temperature coefficient is strongly negative and more so at lower temperatures (See figure 3.3 in Ref. 48). Since changes in the fuel temperature follow closely after changes in the power level it produces a rapid effect on reactivity. This provides an important contribution to short term reactor stability since it moves to quench increases in the neutron population.

Increases in the moderator temperature shift the energy of thermal neutrons to slightly higher values which decreases the thermal neutron fission cross-section of U-235 and thus reduces thermal utilisation in U-235. For Pu-239, which grows in as a fuel is used up, there is a broad fission resonance at 0.3 eV. Increases in moderator temperature make fission of Pu-239 much more likely and this can produce a positive moderator coefficient in reactors with more used fuel. Moderator temperature depends on the amount of heating it is getting from the fuel and from nuclear reactions within it and on the amount of cooling from the cooling circuits. Its temperature moves more slowly than the temperature of fuel so this coefficient is

---

[26] Resonance absorption happens when the energy provided by an incident neutron (binding energy + kinetic energy) exactly matches the energy level of an excited state of the resulting compound nucleus because the system does not have to cope with an energy mismatch. See Section B.3.

more slowly acting.

This section has presented the principles of coefficients of reactivity. The following section concentrates on those that matter most to the Chernobyl story.

4.3.3.2. Coolant Void Coefficient

The coolant void coefficient that dominated the Chernobyl reactor's positive feedback is seen as the major design flaw in the reactor and the principle cause of the accident.

A reactor cooled by boiling water contains a certain amount of steam in its core. The steam bubbles are called voids, and that proportion of the coolant volume which consists of voids is called the void fraction.

Because of the large graphite to fuel ratio in the RBMK reactor the graphite produces a well thermalized neutron spectrum without a significant contribution from the cooling water. This was a design choice to avoid having to significantly enrich the fuel in U-235 (Ref. 50).

Changing the density of the water-steam mixture by changing the voidage fraction therefore has little effect on the level of moderation in the reactor. It does, however, affect the absorption of neutrons. More water and less steam results in more absorption of neutrons and the reduction in reactivity. Since more steam is formed when the power level is increased the coolant void coefficient is positive (power increases lead to changes (more steam) that produce more power increases).

As the relative importance of the absorption of neutrons in the cooling circuit depends to a certain extent on the absence or presence of other absorbers, the magnitude and sign of this term depends upon the void fraction, the control rod positions, the fuel enrichment, the fuel burn-up and absorber loading. Thus this term varies over time and can also vary quite significantly over the volume of the reactor.

It seems that what happened at Chernobyl was that there were very few absorbers in the core, particularly low down in the core, immediately before the accident. This includes control rods used for general management of the reactivity across the core and special absorbing rods placed in the reactor to counterbalance the presence of new fuel. As a result, a larger fraction of the absorption of neutrons than was healthy was taking place in the cooling water. When the water was removed by the formation of steam voids a large increase of reactivity took place. NUREG 1250 (Ref. 51) claims that the void coefficient was probably about 1.5 times its usual value because so many control rods were out at the time of the accident.

There is a claim that the steam-void coefficient could have been as high as 5β where β is the delayed neutron fraction (Ref. 32). As discussed later (Section B.1) a reactivity addition of greater than β is too high.

After the accident the remaining RBMK reactors were made safer by adding more absorbers (increasing *parasitic absorption*) and then increasing the enrichment of the fuel (increasing the thermal utilisation factor) to compensate. In doing so the relative effect of changes in the void fraction were reduced to more manageable levels.

The important thing to take from this section is that, at the time of the accident, the reactor was unusually and dangerously sensitive to the voidage fraction in the cooling water circuits. At the same time, as we will see later, this parameter was unusually sensitive to the rate of pumping and the water inlet temperature.

4.3.3.3. Graphite temperature coefficient

Increasing the graphite temperature "hardens" the neutron spectrum (moves it to higher energies) which:
- decreases absorption in the water (which increases reactivity);
- increases resonance absorption by U-238 (which reduces reactivity); and
- increases fissions in plutonium (which increases reactivity, particularly in well used fuel).

The graphite temperature coefficient becomes more positive as the fuel is burned-up due to increasing amounts of fissile plutonium the fuel.

Just before the accident the graphite in the Chernobyl 4 reactor was subjected to an unusual set of circumstances (low reactor power and high pumping rates) and was therefore at an unusually low graphite temperature. This would have reduced reactivity.

Just before the accident the graphite in the Chernobyl reactor was colder than usual, reducing the overall reactivity of the core.

4.3.3.4. Fuel Temperature Coefficient

The fuel temperature coefficient for a RBMK is negative because Doppler broadening of the resonance absorption peaks increases absorption in U-238 with increasing temperature. However, it becomes less negative as the fuel is burned up and in-grown plutonium makes a greater contribution to the total number of fissions. On the day of the accident the Chernobyl core had a high burn-up reducing the negative fuel coefficient.

This coefficient is more negative at higher temperatures and, since fuel temperature is related to reactor power, it is more negative at high power. At the time of the accident the Chernobyl reactor was running at low power, further reducing the fuel coefficient (making it less negative). But remember that the fuel temperature responds very quickly to changes in power so the resonance absorption in the fuel would increase rapidly as the fuel heated up.

Just before the accident the fuel temperature coefficient was negative but smaller than usual.

4.3.3.5. Power coefficient

The power coefficient relates changes in power to changes in reactivity. An increase in reactor power will cause temperatures to rise and densities to drop unless adjustments are made. The power coefficient therefore depends on how the temperatures and densities of the fuel, moderator and coolant change and on how the reactivity depends on these parameters. These temperature and pressure changes have different time frames with fuel changes having a faster impact than moderator and coolant changes.

A reactor with a negative power coefficient will be self-correcting and inherently stable. A rise in power density at any position in the reactor will tend to damp itself out. With a positive power coefficient there is a need for controls to make continual adjustments in order to maintain constant power levels.

Under normal operating conditions the RBMK's power coefficient is slightly negative because the negative fuel temperature coefficient is just sufficient to outweigh the positive void coefficient. As the power level is decreased both the fuel and void coefficients increase in magnitude but still have opposite signs. At power levels below about 20% of full power the power coefficient becomes positive (Ref. 50).

Physical process	Effect		Time constant (s)
	Stabilising	Destabilising	
Fuel temperature reactivity feedback	x		5 -12
Void reactivity feedback		x	1 - 5
Moderator temperature reactivity feedback		x	$60 - 10^4$
Xenon concentration reactivity feedback		x	$10^4 - 10^5$
Delayed neutron		x	1 - 2000
Neutron leakage	x		$10^{-4} - 10^{-2}$
Prompt neutron		x	10^{-3}

Table 6 RBMK relative time constants for changes

The important thing to take from this section is that the reactivity of a reactor is sensitive to temperatures and pressures.

Before the accident the reactivity of the reactor at Chernobyl was unusually sensitive to the amount of steam in the coolant circuit. More steam, less water, would increase the reactivity.

The reactor had an unusually large positive power coefficient -any increase in power would initiate changes that would further increase the power.

4.3.4.   Delayed neutrons and prompt criticality

It is important to understand the difference between prompt and delayed neutrons and that reactors can be controlled when the continuation of the chain reaction (criticality) depends on the contribution of delayed neutrons. If the situation is reached where the number of prompt neutrons resulting in further fissions is greater than one there will be an uncontrollably rapid increase in reactor power: it will explode.

Understanding the mathematics and the details of delayed neutron production, which is given in more detail in Section B.1, is optional.

In previous sections we discussed the multiplication factor and reactivity of the reactor. These are two ways of describing how the number of neutrons change between generations of the chain reaction. What we have not discussed is the time between generations.

Very important for reactor control and of note with regard to the Chernobyl accident is the existence of *delayed neutrons.* These are neutrons emitted by the decay of fission fragments sometime after the fission takes place.

An example of a delayed neutron source is I-137 which is a fission fragment (about 3.5% of thermal fissions of U-235 produce I-137). It decays with a half-life of 24.5 seconds and has a βn decay to Xe-136 with a branching ratio of about 7% (Ref. 52). This means that 7% of the occurrences of an I-137 fission fragment would decay by giving out a beta particle and a neutron. Thus, on average each fission produces about 2.5×10^{-3} delayed neutrons with a production half-life of 24.5 seconds via this route[27].

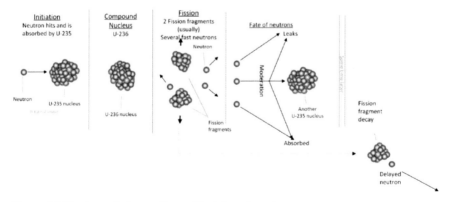

Figure 11 Neutron chain reaction with delayed neutrons

---

[27] For brevity this treatment has ignored any reactions between the I-137 and the neutron field.

Although there are many fission fragments that release delayed neutrons it is usual to treat them as coming from a small number of groups. Traditionally 6 groups of delayed neutrons are recognised[28]. These groups are characterised by a half-life and by the number of delayed fissions per fission in the group (Table 7). It should be noted that these half-lives, and the resulting mean delay time between the original fission and the emission of the delayed neutron are very large compared to the lifetime (slowing down time + diffusion time) of a prompt neutron (Table 8).

Delayed neutrons are produced at a range of energies that are generally lower than those of neutrons produced directly by the fission process. As a result of this they are more likely to survive resonance absorption and are more likely to induce another fission than are fission neutrons. This can be accounted for in mathematical models of the reactor by a suitable inflation of the number of delayed neutrons in the equations.

For U-235 the fraction of delayed neutrons is about 0.0065. For Pu-239 it is 0.0021. Because of this, and the fact that Pu-239 is produced in reactor cores as they age, the delayed neutron factor can vary with fuel composition[29] and burn-up[30].

The importance of delayed neutrons for reactor control can be demonstrated by considering what the situation would be without them.

For an RBMK with a burn-up of 10.3 MWd/kg (towards the end of the fuel's life as at Chernobyl on the day of the accident) the delayed neutron fraction is about 0.0048 and the prompt neutron lifetime is about 0.77 ms (Ref. 51). Now, consider a reactor for which the generation time is 7.7×10^{-4} seconds (0.77 ms) and for which a control rod movement increases k from 1 to 1.001. This means that the neutron flux and the reactor power will increase by a factor of 1.001 every 7.7×10^{-4} seconds. After one

---

[28] The use of six groups is a little bit arbitrary but it was apparently found to be the minimum number of groups to adequately fit early data taken at Los Alamos (Ref. 54).

[29] Some reactors are loaded with fuels that contain Pu-239. MOX (Mixed Oxide Fuel) is a blend of plutonium and uranium oxides using plutonium recovered from used fuels. (Ref. 55)
[30] Burn-up is a measure of how used a fuel element is. The units used are the number of megawatt.days of energy that have been extracted from each kilogramme of fuel.

second the power will have increased by a factor of 1.001 to the power $(1/7.7 \times 10^{-4})$ or 3.7. You cannot control a reactor that can increase in power at this rate![31]

Now consider a reactor with a total fraction β of the neutrons being delayed spread across the 6 groups shown in Table 7. We can see that the average lifetime (cycle period) of a system with prompt and delayed neutrons is given by:

Group	Possible precursor	Half-life s	Number of fission neutrons delayed per fission	Effective yield β_i
1	^{87}Br	55.72	0.00052	0.00021
2	^{137}I	22.72	0.00346	0.00141
3	^{89}Br	6.22	0.00310	0.00127
4	^{139}I	2.30	0.00624	0.00255
5	^{83}As	0.610	0.00182	0.00074
6	^{9}Li	0.230	0.00066	0.00027
Total delayed			0.00158	0.00645
Total fission neutrons			2.42	
Fraction delayed			0.0065	

Table 7 Delayed neutron groups for U-235 (Ref. 53)

Moderator	Slowing down time (s)	Diffusion time (s)
Water	5.6×10^{-6}	2.1×10^{-4}
Heavy water	4.3×10^{-5}	1.4×10^{-1}
Beryllium	5.7×10^{-5}	3.9×10^{-3}
Graphite	1.5×10^{-4}	1.7×10^{-2}

Table 8 Neutron lifetimes in common moderators - data from Ref. 53.

---

[31] At this rate of increase it would take the output of a candle (about 80W) about 15 seconds to reach the current total generation of electricity in the UK (37.826 GW at the time of writing) (Ref. 56). Time= $7.7 \times 10^{-4} \times \frac{\ln(37.826 \times 10^9 / 80)}{\ln(1.001)}$

$$l_p (1 - \beta) + \sum_{i=1}^{6} l_i \beta_i$$

Where:

l_p is the prompt neutron lifetime (s)

l_i is the delayed neutron lifetime of group i (s) which is dominated by the half-life of the precursor.

β_i is the delayed neutron fraction for group i

If we take l_p to be 7.7 x 10^{-4} s and the values for delayed neutrons given in Table 7, we get an average delayed neutron lifetime of about 13 seconds and an average cycle time of 0.08 seconds.

If we look at the example of a jump in k from 1 to 1.001 as before, but this time use a cycle time of 0.08 seconds the reactor power at time t (seconds) is given by $1.001^{(t/0.08)}$. After 1 second the reactor power is 1.01. This time it takes about 70 seconds for the reactor power to double. This is much more controllable.

If we increase the reactivity to the extent that the reactor is critical without the neutron contribution from the longest lived precursor the average delayed neutron lifetime reduces to 10.7 seconds (by running the summation from 2 to 6 instead of 1 to 6). Extending this to the remaining groups gives average delayed lifecycle times of 4.3s, 2.5s and 0.73s compared to 13s when all delayed neutrons play their part.

As the reactor approaches prompt criticality (the condition where the delayed neutrons are not required to keep the chain reaction going) the cycle time drops dramatically and the reactor becomes increasingly unstable; prone to rapid increases in power in response to small injections of added reactivity.

It can be shown that if a reactor that is critical with prompt and delayed neutrons and a small insertion of reactivity is made then the reactor power will experience a relatively rapid jump in power followed by a slower but continuing exponential rise. The first component is due to prompt neutrons and the second to delayed neutrons. See Figure 12, which is discussed in more detail in Section B.1.

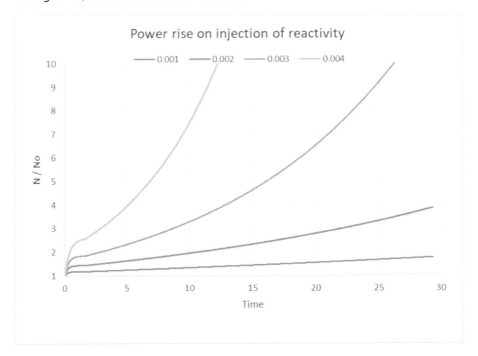

Figure 12 Reactor power rise (neutron population) on injection of reactivity

Delayed neutrons make reactor control possible but they complicate reactor analysis because it is necessary to model the change in the concentrations of the neutron emitters with time following a reactivity change and the effects of neutrons with a range of energies being emitted during a range of times following the initial fission. In real reactors these parameters can all vary with burn-up.

The important message to take from this section is that small increments in reactivity within a critical reactor assembly are controllable because of time delay for the delayed neutrons. As reactivity rises the delayed neutrons matter less and the cycle time reduces giving less time for controls to be effective. As reactivity rises to the point at which the reactor is critical on prompt neutrons alone the reactor becomes dangerously unstable. A small insertion of additional reactivity will yield a prompt super-critical reactor which will increase its power output very rapidly: it will be out of control, it will explode.

4.3.5.   Neutron poisons

Neutron poisons are isotopes that have an unusually large cross section for the absorption of neutrons. We use these in control rods to provide the capability to increase or decrease the reactivity on demand, we use them in distributed absorbers used to control the neutron flux shape across the reactor and hold-down new fuel which would otherwise be too reactivity for the control rods.

Importantly some fission fragments are also neutron poisons and they can have a significant at changing effect on reactivity.

The fission process produces a range of fission fragments with different nuclear properties although they all tend to be neutron rich and therefore beta/gamma active. Some of the fission fragments also have large thermal neutron capture cross sections. This means that they are very likely to absorb a thermal neutron and thus prevent it from being able to initiate a fission; they decrease the thermal utilisation factor.

One such notable neutron poison that played a part in the Chernobyl accident is Xe-135. This is produced as fission fragment and from the decay of other fission fragments (I-135 and Te-135). It has an extremely large neutron capture cross section. When it captures a neutron it is removed from the system along with the neutron. It is also beta/gamma active with a half-life of 9.2 hours.

Interesting first-hand accounts of the confirmation of the role of Xe-135 in reactor poisoning can be found in Refs. 57 & 58.

We can illustrate the production and removal of these nuclei as shown in Figure 13.

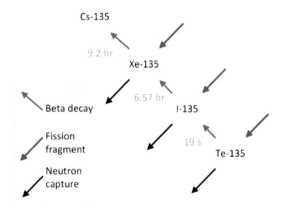

Figure 13 Production and destruction of Xe-135

The cumulative fission fragment yields for thermal fission of U-235 are I-135 6.39+/-0.22, Xe-135 6.61+/-0.22 (IAEA Ref. 59). For the sake of simplicity we will ignore Te-135 and fold its contribution into the fission fragment yield of I-135.

The differential equation for the rate of change of the concentration of Xe-135 nuclei with time is:

$$\frac{d}{dt} N_{Xe} = Y_{Xe}.\Sigma_f.\phi + \lambda_I.N_I - \lambda_{Xe}.N_{Xe} - \sigma_a^{Xe}.N_{Xe}.\phi$$

Where:

$Y_{Xe}.\Sigma_f.\phi$ Production of Xe-135 from fission.

$\lambda_I.N_I$ Production of Xe-135 from the decay of I-135.

$\lambda_{Xe}.N_{Xe}$ Loss of Xe-135 due to radioactive decay.

$\sigma_a^{Xe}.N_{Xe}.\phi$ Loss of Xe-135 by neutron capture (burn out).

You will note that there is one term for each arrow (process) in the diagram above.

And for Iodine:

$$\frac{d}{dt} N_I = Y_I'.\Sigma_f.\phi - \lambda_I.N_I - \sigma_a^I.N_I.\phi$$

With

Y_{Xe} Fission fragment yield of Xe-135   (0.003)

Y_I Cumulative Fission fragment yield of I-135 (0.061)

Σ_f Macroscopic thermal fission cross section of the fuel (cm^2)

ϕ Neutron flux   ($cm^{-2}.s^{-1}$)

λ_{Xe} Decay constant for Xe-135 ($2.1 \times 10^{-5}\,s^{-1}$)

λ_I Decay constant for I-135 ($2.9 \times 10^{-5}s^{-1}$)

N_{Xe} Number density of Xe-135 nuclei (cm^{-3})

N_I Number density of I-135 nuclei (cm^{-3})

σ_a^{Xe} Cross section for absorbtion of thermal neutron by Xe-135 (3.0×10^6 b)

σ_a^I Cross section for absorbtion of thermal neutron by I-135

These equations can be solved but some insight can be gained just by looking at the equilibrium situation and how changes in reactivity might affect it.

If the reactor has been running at the same power level of long enough the concentrations of I-135 and Xe-135 will not change with time (the rate of production will be equal to the rate of destructon).

$$\frac{d}{dt} N_I = Y_I'.\Sigma_f.\phi - \lambda_I.N_I - \sigma_a^I.N_I.\phi = 0$$

From which:

$$N_I(\text{equilibrium}) = \frac{Y_I'.\Sigma_f.\phi}{\lambda_I + \sigma_a^I.\phi} \sim \frac{Y_I'.\Sigma_f.\phi}{\lambda_I}$$

Since σ_a^I is relatively small. So equilibrium I-135 levels are proportional to neutron flux (if the flux is high enough) (Figure 14).

Now putting this into the first equation and setting that equal to zero gives:

$$Y_{Xe}.\Sigma_f.\phi + Y_I'.\Sigma_f.\phi - \lambda_{Xe}.N_{Xe} - \sigma_a^{Xe}.N_{Xe}.\Phi = 0$$

From which:

$$N_{Xe}(\text{equilibrium}) = \frac{(Y_{Xe} + Y_I').\Sigma_f.\phi}{\lambda_{Xe} + \sigma_a^{Xe}.\phi}$$

At high enough fluxes (such that $\lambda_{Xe} \ll \sigma_a^{Xe}.\phi$) this reaches a constant given by $\frac{(Y_{Xe} + Y_I').\Sigma_f}{\sigma_a^{Xe}}$, thereafter increases in flux do not lead to a significant change in the levels of Xe-135 (Figure 14).

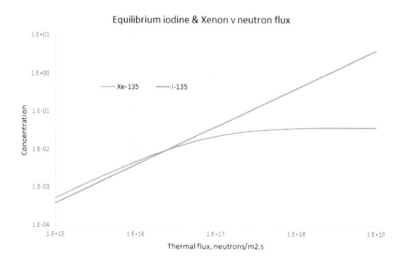

Figure 14 Equilibrium iodine and xenon v neutron flux

It can be shown that the reactivity equivalent $\Delta\rho_0$ of the equilibrium xenon poisoning effect is given by $\Delta\rho_0 \sim \dfrac{-N_{Xe,0}\sigma_{Xe}}{\Sigma_a}$.

A plot of this is shown as Figure 15.

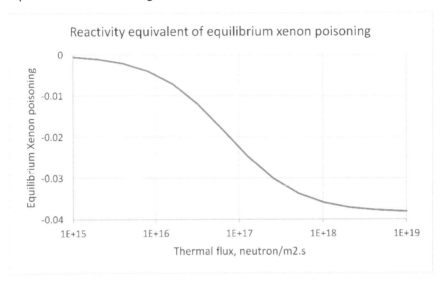

Figure 15 Reactivity equivalent of equilibrium xenon poisoning

See Ref. 60 for a clear analysis of neutron poisons in CANDU reactors.

4.3.5.1. Xenon levels during shutdown from power run

Most of the xenon-135 in the reactor is formed from the decay of I-135. Therefore the instantaneous production rate of xenon-135 is dependent on the iodine-135 concentration and therefore on the local <u>neutron flux history</u>. On the other hand, the destruction rate of xenon-135 is dependent on the <u>instantaneous local neutron flux</u>.

When a reactor is shutdown from a power run the neutron flux reduces to near zero so the production of I-135 and Xe-135 from the fission process stops as does the neutron induced burnout. For a while Xe-135 will still be produced by the decay of I-135 and the Xe-135 will decay by beta decay. The equations governing these are:

$$\frac{d}{dt}N_{Xe} = -\lambda_{Xe}N_{Xe} + \lambda_I N_I$$

$$\frac{d}{dt}N_{Xe} = -\lambda_{Xe}N_{Xe} + \lambda_I N_{I,o}e^{-\lambda_I t}$$

Solving this gives:

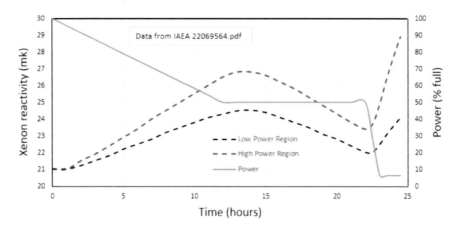

Figure 16 Chernobyl, modelled xenon transient

$$N_{Xe}(t) = \frac{\lambda_I}{\lambda_{Xe} - \lambda_I}\, N_{I,0}\,(\exp(-\lambda_I t) - \exp(-\lambda_{Xe}t)) + N_{Xe,0}(\exp(-\lambda_I t))$$

If a reactor, that has been operating for a sufficient time for the Xe-135 and I-135 to have reached equilibrium, suddenly drops in power then the rate of destruction of Xe-135 will reduce in proportion to the power with no time lag while the rate of production will reduce more slowly as the I-135 moves towards its new lower equilibrium level. Thus the level of Xe-135, and its negative effect on reactivity, will increase at first, then decrease as the levels of I-135 decrease, reaching a new lower equilibrium. The peak of this "xenon transient" is at about 11 hours after the power change.

Figure 16 shows an attempt to model the Xenon transient in the Chernobyl accident (Data taken from Ref. 61). It shows the xenon building up as the power is reduced from full power to 50% power, reducing during the waiting stage and then rising rapidly when the power levels accidently dropped and were slow to recover.

For the Chernobyl accident, it is believed that the reactor had a large axial power density difference (the axial power peaking factor is given as 1.4 in Table 1). This means a higher power density in the middle than at the top and bottom. The Xenon transient that resulted from the inadvertent drop to zero power produced significant poisoning of the middle region of the reactor effectively separating the neutron fields at the top and the bottom of the reactor from each other.

The important thing to take from this section is that the fission product Xe-135 (there are a few others) is an important neutron poison that reaches an equilibrium concentration (and effect) if a reactor operates at a constant power level for long enough (about half a day). If you suddenly reduce the power level then the Xe-135 level will increase for several hours, reducing the reactivity of your core by absorbing neutrons, before decaying away. This is the Xenon transient or iodine pit.

5. Relevant aspects of reactor design and operation

This section will look at some of the aspects of the design and operation of the Chernobyl reactor that are relevant to the accident.

5.1. Control rod design

The control rods in the Chernobyl reactor have come in for a lot of criticism. There is little doubt that they played an important part in the accident. This description has largely been taken from INSAG-7 (Ref. 13) and Malko (Ref. 32).

Apart from 24 shortened absorbing rods (SAR) which are inserted from the bottom of the reactor to control the axial shape of the power distribution the control rods are inserted from the top of the reactor. There were:

- 139 absorbing rods for the manual regulating of the radial neutron distribution (MR);
- 24 absorbing rods for the auto-control of the reactor power (AC);
- 24 emergency rods (ER).

The control rods consist of boron carbide elements of 967.5 mm length. The shortened absorbing rods have three of these elements and a total length of 3,050 mm. The other rods have 5 boron carbide elements and length 5,120 mm. The SAR, MR and ER rods have graphite displacers below them with a total length of 4.5m. These improve the neutron economy in normal operation since without them the volume below the control rods would be filled with water which would absorb more neutrons than the graphite displacers. They also help the control rods move into the reactor more smoothly.

When the SAR, MR or ER rods are fully withdrawn from the reactor the graphite displacers are in the middle of the reactor with 1.25m of water above and below them[32]. (The reactor height is 7m). When they are fully inserted the graphite displacers are below the core and the boron carbide is centred in the core with water above and below.

---

[32] NUREG 1250 (Ref. 51) has this measurement as 1m.

Moving a rod inwards from its fully out position displaces neutron-absorbing water with graphite in the lower part of the core until the rods has travelled 1.25m and the strongly neutron-absorbing boron carbide elements come into place at the top of the reactor. This causes a power rise at the bottom of the reactor. The effect was known to operators as the "end-rods effect" and to specialists as the "positive reactivity surge".

Under normal insertion conditions the Chernobyl rods moved at 0.4 m.s^{-1} and thus could be travelling for 18 - 20 seconds before they reach the bottom of the reactor[33] (to travel 7 m at 0.4 m.s^{-1} takes 17.5 seconds).

Looking at Figure 17 you can see that if a rod was inserted from fully extracted it would first replace water with boron carbide in region 1 at the top of the reactor reducing reactivity; replace graphite with water in region 2 near the top of the reactor reducing reactivity; but, and very importantly, replace water with graphite in region 3 near the bottom of the reactor adding reactivity. This addition of reactivity near the bottom of the reactor played an important role in the power surge.

5.2. Power Control

There were two main power control systems in the Chernobyl reactor on the day of the accident.

The system that INSAG-7 calls the Physical Power Density Distribution Control System (PPDDCS) has detectors inside the core while the Reactor Control System (RCS) has detectors located inside the core as well as outside the core in the lateral biological shield tank.

The PPDDCS was designed to control the relative and absolute power output of zones within the reactor and to control the total reactor power. This is achieved by dividing the reactor into twelve zones each of which has a number of neutron rate meters and a control rod. If the local power is seen to be creeping too high or too low the system gently moves the control rod to compensate. To change the total power output of the reactor all, or many, of the rods would be moved together. This system was used at power levels above 10%.

At lower power the reactor operators were dependent solely on ex-core detectors which could tell them nothing about the power distribution within the core. Nor could the ex-core detectors give any information on the axial distribution since they were all on the mid-plane of the reactor. While operators had experience of this with fresh cores being powered-up for the first time there was little or no operating

---

[33] This is a relatively slow insertion time. The soviets claim that the low speed is compensated by the number of control rods (Ref. 29).

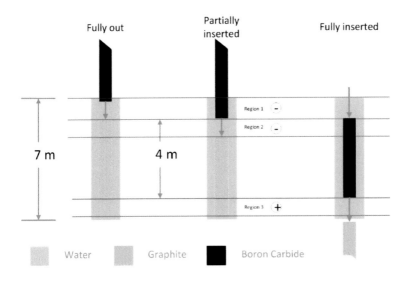

Figure 17 *Control rods in Chernobyl reactor*

experience with heavy burned-up and poisoned cores with their complex, and changing, reactivity distributions.

These control systems played their part in the accident in that when the operator switched from local to global power control the reactor output plummeted to effectively nothing. This has been blamed on operator error, on equipment malfunction and on poor design in different reports. It triggered a xenon transient and the operators struggled to bring the power levels back to where the experiment could be undertaken.

5.3. Power distribution

In a nuclear reactor the bulk of the heat is generated where a fissile nucleus (the fuel, generally U-235) is hit by a neutron (usually a slow neutron). The distribution of heat output therefore depends on the layout of the fuel and the neutron flux across the reactor.

In the middle of the reactor the fuel experiences neutrons coming at it from all directions. Near the edges that is not true; there are some directions, those outside the core, from which no neutrons come other than neutrons reflected by the materials beyond the core. This means that the neutron flux is lower at the edges of the core and so, if all else is the same, power density will be lower, the fuel will be used more slowly and the channel will be cooler. This causes problems for the reactor designers and operators who are trying to extract as much heat from the reactor as possible and who wish to use all the fuel to its maximum benefit but are limited to a maximum channel temperature or power. Thus designers and operators have to go to some lengths to "flatten" the neutron flux profile to reduce the difference between the hottest and coldest channel by varying the fuel and poison composition across the core. They also have to reduce the coolant flow through the cooler parts of the core to maintain steam quality.

For a clear description of the power density in a finite cylindrical reactor see Ref. 62.

It is important to note that the RBMK reactor core is significantly bigger than the mean path length of a fission neutron. The result of this is that different parts of the core can have different neutron density and different reactivity.

5.4. Operating Reactivity Margin (ORM)

Many commentaries on the Chernobyl accident cite the fact that the reactor breached the permitted limits for Operating Reactivity Margin (ORM) in the period leading up to the accident as a lead cause of the accident and clearly blame the operators for this occurring. However, the term is not always well explained and its role in the accident can be unclear.

The Operating Reactivity Margin (ORM) is a measure of the value (reactivity) of the control rods and other absorbers inserted into the reactor and is expressed in units of "equivalent control rods". It is therefore a measure of the reactivity that would be added to the core if all of the control rods and absorbers were withdrawn. There were rules setting minimum levels of ORM at Chernobyl; the operators were not allowed to go below 26 rods equivalent without the authorisation of the Chief Engineer and if the value reached 15 or less the reactor was to be shut down immediately.

Operating reactivity margin is required to allow the system to adjust for reduced fuel reactivity as it burns up (which uses up the fissile U-235 and adds neutron poisoning fission fragments), to allow power density across the reactor to be controlled and to compensate for the xenon transient, allowing a reactor to be restarted promptly after a power reduction transient. ORM can be provided by control rods or by poisons such as boron in the cooling water, inserted absorber bars or burnable poisons incorporated into new fuel. These aspects of ORM are about the ability to operate the reactor efficiently, they are not primarily safety considerations.

In essence, if you run out of operational reactivity margin (controllable poisons in the reactor) you lose the ability to affect the shape of the neutron flux density within the reactor, leading to inefficient situations; you lose the ability to climb out of the Xenon transient; and you lose the ability to counterbalance reducing reactivity in the fuel as it burns up. Usually this means that it is time to refuel the reactor.

In the Chernobyl reactors the positioning of control rods had two additional safety significances that the shift operators might not have been aware of. The first was that the presence of absorbers in the core reduced the relative importance of absorption in the cooling water and hence reduced the sensitivity to coolant voidage. The second was that design faults that meant that the rod movement was rather slow and that if the rods were fully withdrawn they actually added reactivity to a region of the core for a period of time when they started to move inwards.

Ten years after the accident L. Lederman, writing for the IAEA explained that "*the safety significance of the safety issue related to the operational reactivity margin (ORM) is high since the ORM has to be controlled in order to maintain the void reactivity coefficient, the effectiveness of the shutdown system (insertion rate, shutdown subcriticality) and the power distribution within the given safety limits*" (Ref. 63). It is not clear if this was known by the operators on the night of the accident.

INSAG-7 seems to reluctantly agree with this suggestion "*According to the record, the computer SKALA, which was used to calculate the ORM, became unreliable in the period in which the test took place. In the view of INSAG, it is likely that the operator did not know the value of the ORM during the critical part of the test. Probably he was aware that continued operation under conditions of increasing xenon content of the reactor was reducing the ORM. The operators had been accustomed to regarding the lower limit on ORM as necessary for control of the reactor's spatial power distribution, but were not aware that it had safety significance by virtue of the increase in positive void coefficient as the ORM was reduced. Nor were they sensitized to the need to retain a suitable number of control or safety rods in a partially inserted position, for fast reactivity decrease if necessary. In fact, the safety significance of the reduction of the ORM is much greater than was indicated in the INSAG-1 report*" (INSAG-7 Ref. 13).

Measurement of ORM is quite complex and the system to do it at Chernobyl gave results 10 to 15 minutes behind real time and at a console some distance from the Operators' area. This suggests that it was seen as an operational tool to provide long term understanding of the reactor rather than to be watched with the care due to a safety parameter.

Because of the reactor power manoeuvres leading up to the accident almost all of the control rods were out of the reactor and the ORM limits breached. But it is likely that the operators were not aware of this as the build up to the experiment progressed. Indeed, the senior officer on the night of the accident, Anatoly Dyatlov, is quoted as saying "*The Chernobyl operating staff made a mistake on 26 April in having over-looked the reduction of the ORM below the level of 15 rods stipulated in the regulations. Although the staff were not aware of the significance of the ORM in* terms of its capability to transform the emergency protection system into a reactor excursion device, they were not exactly treating this parameter lightly. Controlling power density distribution is always a serious business. A violation here can lead to a major accident" (Ref. 31).

In the final analysis it was not the low value of ORM that helped destroy the reactor. It was not even the fact that so many control rods were fully retracted. What helped destroy the reactor was that when the button was pressed to scram the reactor an unusually large number of rods started to travel into the reactor and, bizarrely, each one of them added a little bit of reactivity at its leading edge instead of immediately providing negative reactivity as they should have done. At the same time the absence of the control rods had made the reactor very sensitive to the void fraction and that was about to change dramatically (or already had done so a few moments earlier).

5.5. Thermal hydraulics

This section concentrates on the reactor cooling system which played an important role in the accident.

5.5.1. Primary Coolant Circuit

Page 104 of INSAG-7 has a detailed and informative diagram of the primary coolant circuit at Chernobyl of which Figure 18 is a significant simplification. In particular, this diagram does not show the number of pressure vessels, pumps or valves in the reactor system nor the condensate treatment and reheating apparatus between the condensers and the feed pumps.

The RBMK reactor is cooled by two independent loops, each cooling half of the fuel channels in the reactor. This is a complex plumbing system, consisting of electrically powered main coolant pumps feeding a common manifold and then 22 distributor headers in each half which, in turn feed the 1661 coolant channels in the reactor. There are four main coolant pumps on each half. Three of these at a time are used in normal operation with the fourth being a back-up.

Each main coolant pump has a flow control valve, and a check valve to prevent back-flow on their outlet side and a shutoff valve to isolate it. Each channel has a flow control valve to throttle the flow into the channel in order to allow control of the radial power distribution[34].

---

[34] At the edge of the reactor, where there is leakage to consider, the neutron density and hence power density is lower than in the middle of the reactor. This means that the channels will be relatively cool. To ensure that steam quality is maintained the coolant flow in these channels is

The pumps have massive fly wheels to provide rotational inertia in the event of electricity supply disruption. It takes these pumps about 16 seconds to get from stand-still to full rotation speed and 2 - 5 minutes to stop (Ref. 64).

The normal core inlet temperature is 270°C and the core outlet temperature is 284°C at a pressure of 7 Mpa (approximately 70 atm) (INSAG-7, Ref. 13).

The turbines can be isolated and the steam diverted into the condensers through pressure reducing valves (Ref. 33).

The steam-water mixture is transferred by individual pipes to steam separators (two per loop, these are large - nearly 3m in diameter and 30m long). Steam exits the top of these devices to drive turbines while the water is mixed with the condensate from the turbines (delivered by a system that filters and de-aerates it with 7 main feed water pumps and a number of auxiliary pumps for start-up and emergency standby) and then returned to the main coolant pumps. Thus the steam separators have three roles: the separation of the steam from the steam water mixture from the reactor; the mixing of water from the condensers (feed water) with the water separated out from the steam[35]; and acting as a buffer store for water to feed the main coolant pumps on demand.

The water in the suction headers (inlets) of the main coolant pumps is therefore a mixture of the water component of the steam/water mixture leaving the reactor and the relatively cold condensate being pumped back from the condensers under the turbines. Its temperature is therefore a function of the reactor outlet temperature, flow and steam quality and the volume and temperature of water returning from the turbines, which in turn is affected by the energy removed by the turbine and generator.

---

slowed using valves to throttle the flow. As well as improving stream quality this process raises the voidage in the channel which decreases neutron absorption and helps increase the channel power. Other tricks to level the power across the reactor include increasing the enrichment of fuel at the edges of the reactor, reducing control rods and poisons and putting a reflector outside the reactor.

[35] This mixing affects the temperature of water to the main coolant pumps.

5.5.2.   Impact of reactor power reduction

A reduction in reactor power will reduce the energy being generated in the fuel. Unless the flow of coolant water is reduced the steam quality will suffer leading to more direct recycling of hot water to the coolant pump intakes, less energy extraction by the turbines and a narrowing of the temperature difference between

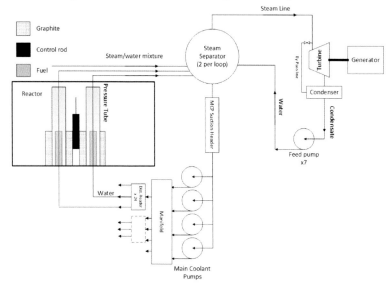

Figure 18 Chernobyl cooling circuit (Simplified)

the water leaving the reactor at the top and re-entering the reactor at the bottom. Generally at low power fewer pumps are used and the throttles limit flow to keep pump inlet temperatures below the cavitation range.

5.5.3.   Sub-cooling

Subcooling is the difference in water temperature in the drum separators, where steam and water exist together at the boiling point of water at that pressure, and at the core inlet. It is therefore related to the amount of sensible heat the reactor must add to the coolant flow to induce boiling. All other things being equal, the smaller this number, the lower in the core cooling will occur.

In the RBMK reactors water is pumped into the bottom of the core *sub-cooled* below the boiling point of water at that pressure. It is heated as it passes up the hot core and boiling begins at some distance along the flow path. The degree of sub-cooling is important for reactor stability. If it is too low, approaching zero, then the water boils almost at the core inlet increasing the *void fraction* (the fraction of the in-core cooling system that is steam bubble rather than water) and decreasing the amount of neutron absorption in the cooling circuit. The void fraction also affects viscosity, pressure drop and heat transfer. It is harder to pump a water/steam mixture through pipes and orifices than it is to pump the same mass of water. The heat transfer from the fuel to the coolant reduces as the steam quality rises. For some of the complexities of two-phase flow see Ref. 65.

Another danger is that the water will boil in the pumps (cavitation - see Section 5.5.4) leading to reduced pumping efficiency, vibration and pump damage.

5.5.4.   Cavitation

Cavitation is a phenomenon found in pumps where, under certain conditions (including the liquid being near its boiling point), the pressure changes around the pump's impellor leads to the formation and destruction of bubbles causing shockwaves within the pump. See Ref. 66 for a fuller description.

It is said that a pump that is subject to cavitation sounds like a can of marbles being shaken. Other symptoms include:

- Fluctuation in discharge pressure;
- Fluctuations in flow rate;
- Distinctive crackling noise;
- Fluctuations pump motor current;
- Erratic power consumptions;
- Reduction in pump efficiency and output.

All of these are bad news when applied to the main cooling pumps of a nuclear reactor.

5.5.5.   Positive Void Coefficient

Much is made of the positive void coefficient of the Chernobyl Reactor 4 and its key role in the nuclear emergency. Basically as the water/steam mixture is heated it becomes more steam and less water (its void fraction rises and its density drops) and so it absorbs fewer neutrons (leaving more to induce fissions) and power density rises. In summary, making the reactor hotter induces changes that makes it even hotter - a positive feedback mechanism.

Water acts as a neutron "poison," or neutron absorber, because neutrons form deuterium out of the hydrogen in the water molecule.

$$N + {}^{1}_{1}H \rightarrow {}^{2}_{1}H$$

One reason why *heavy water*, in which more of the hydrogen is deuterium (^{2}H), is preferred as a moderator and coolant over normal water is the significant reduction in the absorption of neutrons.

The RBMK is moderated by graphite so changes to the density of water in the coolant circuits has little effect in moderation[36] as opposed to absorption.

It is possible to make a reactor less sensitive to the level of absorption in the coolant circuit by putting in more absorbers so that changes in the void fraction has a relatively reduced significance. The cost of this is that more neutrons are wasted so you have to work harder to achieve criticality.

The RBMK uses enriched fuel to increase the thermal utilisation factor. Additional absorbers separate from the reactor control system are required to counterbalance the reactivity worth of the fuel when it is first loaded but these are removed as the fuel burns up. With these absorbers in place the reactor is less sensitive to the level of absorption in the coolant circuit but as they are removed the void coefficient shifts significantly in the positive direction and is made crucially sensitive to the extent of insertion of the control and protection rods. Thus the void coefficient of the RBMK core depends on a number of factors including the fuel enrichment, the fuel burn-up, the distribution of additional absorbers and the configuration of the control rods.

Nuclear Engineering International (Ref. 67) explain that "*In an RBMK reactor with an 'equilibrium' fuel loading, the magnitude of the positive void effect is sufficient to make the reactor dangerously unstable at powers of 30% full power or lower. At the time of the Chernobyl 4 accident, the reactor's fuel burn-up, control rod configuration and power level combined to place the reactor in an extremely unstable state with a void coefficient so large that it overwhelmed all other influences on the power coefficient*".

Obviously, in situations where the cooling water is doing a greater fraction of the neutron absorption the total reactivity is more sensitive to the void fraction. So in situations where there are a lot of control rods inserted or where there are burnable poisons in place (as when new fuel is loaded) then the void fraction is less important.

It is important to understand that the lack of control rods and absorbers in the reactor made the Chernobyl 4 reactor very sensitivity to the amount of water in the cooling

---

[36] In the PWR the water provides both coolant and moderation in one system. The reactors are designed to be over-moderated. The result of this is that if the power rises and the water gets hotter and therefore less dense it becomes less effective as a moderator. This has a greater impact on reactivity than the reduction in neutron absorption so the nett reactivity is reduced. The system self corrects; it has a negative feedback.

circuits. An increase in the steam content would decrease neutron absorption and add reactivity.

5.5.6.   Thermal instability

When water is being pumped through a reactor at high flow rates it has less time to absorb heat and so the water temperature at a given height will be lower than for slower pumping rates. Any steam bubbles that forms will be tend to be formed higher up the reactor (because of the heat flow) and pushed upwards and out of the reactor more rapidly (because of the high water flow rate). At high water flows voidage is relatively low and relatively stable.

At lower flow rates for the same reactor temperatures, steam bubbles form lower in the reactor and take longer to travel out of the reactor; steam voidage rises. At a low power level a given power increment results in an increase in steam volume in the coolant which is many times more than at nominal full power. This can result in a rapid transition from low to high voidage if the water is close to its boiling point.

Changes in the voidage fraction also affects the work required from the coolant pumps (a water/steam mixture is harder to pump than the same mass as water) and this can feedback and affect the flow rate.

Prior to the accident the Chernobyl reactors were running at low power but with high coolant pumping, an abnormal situation. Coolant flow was significantly above that required for 100% power. This created a nearly solid-water condition in the pressure tubes (almost zero void fraction).

The resulting poor steam quality meant that very little steam was going to drive the turbines and most of the water/steam mixture from the reactor was being recycled to the main coolant pump headers. This reduced the temperature difference between the water entering the reactor and the water leaving the reactor, reducing the sub-cooling of water at the reactor bottom. The difference is quoted as being as low as 3°C (Ref. 32).

The cooling system was in an unstable state where a small change in temperature, pressure or pumping could initiate a rapid change in the voidage fraction, from very low to high. At the same time the reactivity was very sensitive to the voidage fraction.

The accident sequence was going to deliver that small change required to tip the voidage fraction.

Just before the accident the reactors were being cooled with solid water (very little steam) with relatively little temperature difference between the water at the top of the reactor and at the bottom, all of it near to the boiling point. Under these conditions a rapid change to top to bottom boiling is possible.

5.6. Turbines

Turbines are very large pieces of metal (see picture). A typical power plant steam turbine rotates at 1800–3600 rpm (revolutions per minute) so there is some significant stored energy in their rotation. After you stop adding steam to push them they will still turn for a while and you can, in principle at least, still extract some electricity from the generator connected to them.

The important question being asked was "can we using the slowing down turbines to keep the reactor main cooling pumps and feed-water pumps operating sufficiently well until the emergency diesels can take over?

Further reading - Stream Turbines - Ref. 68.

Figure 19 A turbine

5.7. Core cooling and decay heat

Decay heat played no role in the Chernobyl accident but its management was the key concern that led to the fatal experiment. This sub-section is background information.

Nuclear reactors utilise the fission of heavy nuclei to generate heat. While most of energy of fission is produced at the moment of fission about 10% comes from the radioactive decay of fission fragments and their daughter products sometime later. This means that if you suddenly shut the chain reaction down heat will still be being generated from the decay of fission products. The rate of production of decay heat after shutdown from steady state depends on the power history but is of the order of 6% after a second, 3.5% after a minute, 1.2% after an hour and 0.47% after a day. The impact of this heat depends on the power density of the reactor, its heat capacity and its ability to lose heat.

Decay heat production can be modelled using the Wigner-Way formula:

$$P = P_0 \times 0.0622 \; [t^{-0.2} - (t_0 + t)^{-0.2}]$$

Where:

P is the power at time t

P_0 is the steady power level before shutdown

t is the time since shutdown (s)

t_0 is the duration of the power run (s)

Figure 20 shows this equation plotted for reactor run times of 1 day and 1 year (note that this figure is plotted on a log-log scale).

In the RBMK reactor the decay heat is sufficient to cause significant damage so it is important to keep cooling the reactor in such events as a total loss of power to the site. The RBMKs at Chernobyl were supplied with back-up diesel generators to provide the electricity to drive the reactor cooling system. These take time to start-up and take load.

The first line of defence against damage due to loss of cooling in a total loss of power is the Emergency Core Cooling System (ECCS). At Chernobyl the first train of this system consisted of a number of water tanks pressurised with nitrogen. A loss of cooling signal from the reactor protection system would open the valves between these tanks and the cooling circuits pushing water into the cooling circuit and through the reactor. This provides two minutes of cooling. After this further systems pump water into the core from a succession of tanks (Ref. 23). These pumps need electricity and there is a delay while emergency diesel generators are getting up to speed. Electricity from the running down main turbines was expected to fill this gap.

Hence this experiment: "If we lose all power supplies to the site, how much power for cooling can be obtained from the turbines as they spin down and how long is it before we need the backup diesels to be working?"

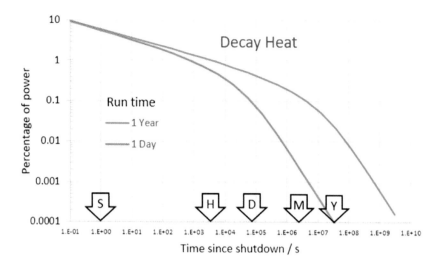

Figure 20 Decay heat estimated using Wigner-Way equation

For more details about decay heat see Section B.6.

6. It all comes together

This section looks again at the timeline of the accident but in more detail and with reference to the physics explained earlier.

6.1. The Chernobyl reactor 4 shift

"As a whole, the Chernobyl personnel in 1986 were characterized as a fairly typical, mature and stable group of specialists with qualifications regarded in the USSR as satisfactory. They were no better, but no worse, than the personnel at other nuclear plants" (INSAG-7).

Plokhy (Ref. 35) describes the people in the control room at Chernobyl in the hours before the accident. The room was fuller than usual with the old shift, the new shift, managers, and engineers from other divisions who were involved in the turbine test or who were there to see how other pieces of equipment behaved during the shut-down. He estimates that there may have been as many as 20 people in the room. Figure 21 shows the control room of the neighbouring reactor taken some years later. This is identical in size and layout to the Reactor 4 control room as used on the day of the accident. Clearly too many people in the room is unhelpful and may hamper the operators.

Notable attendees were Anatolii Diatlov, the deputy chief engineer of the Chernobyl power plant. He was experienced at the site and one of the top nuclear experts there. He was *"known for being difficult, occasionally even rough"*. I've used some of his publications, largely defences of the operators, in this manuscript (Refs. 30 & 31) so it might be worth noting that he spent four years in prison as a result of the accident having been found guilty "*of criminal mismanagement of potentially explosive enterprises*". He suffered 35% burns and absorbed 6 Sv of dose in the aftermath of the accident. He was released on grounds of ill health. His accounts can certainly be considered to be informed but possibly not impartial.

Aleksandr Akimov was the shift lead with ten years of experience on the site but only four months in his current role. Leonid Toptunov was the senior engineer in charge of the reactor's operational regime. His job was to continually adjust an array of controls to keep the reactor balanced. This shift had not expected to be undertaking the experiment. It was the previous shift that had been briefed and had had some time to try and understand the experiment order. Yurii Trehub, the previous shift's lead, had stayed on to help.

In addition to the personnel in the Control Room there would have been further personnel out on plant with duties to monitor and control peripheral equipment and others with maintenance roles.

On the night of 25-26 April 1986 there were 176 duty operational staff and workers from different departments and maintenance services on the operating site and 268 builders and assemblers working on the night shift on the site of the third construction stage (Ref. 29).

6.2. Timeline

6.2.1. Early that day

On 25th April 1986, Reactor 4 was due to be shut down for routine maintenance. It was planned to undertake an electrical test on a turbine during the shutdown to see if, on loss of site power and reactor trip, the turbine could provide enough energy for the core cooling system until the back-up diesels were up and running.

This test had failed the year before but, since then, improved voltage controls had been put in place and it was thought that success was possible. Post-accident it was widely agreed that the test had been poorly conceived and planned and that nuclear safety had not been considered carefully enough.

Figure 21 The Control of Chernobyl Reactor 3 (Photo K.I.Pearce)

The planned start point of the experiment was for the reactor to be at 50% power. At 01:06 power reduction started reaching 1,600 MWt at 03:47 where it was stabilised. This slow change in power level was designed to prevent the build-up of xenon poison and to allow temperatures to change gently.

The emergency core cooling system was disconnected to prevent it interfering with the test. This is not a step to be taken lightly in terms of safety reduction. It is also labour intensive and takes time as many large valves have to be closed manually. This was done at 14:00.

INSAG-7 tells us that *"it was stated in INSAG-1 that blocking of the emergency core cooling system (ECCS) was a violation of procedures. However, later Soviet information confirms that blocking of the ECCS was in fact permissible at Chernobyl if authorized by the Chief Engineer, and that this authorization was given for the tests leading up to the accident and was even an approved step in the test procedure".* Furthermore it states that *"at Chernobyl Unit 4, there was a capability for the operators manually to disable certain safety systems, bypass automatic scram trips, and reset or suppress various alarm signals. This could be done ordinarily by connecting jumper wires to accessible terminals. The operating procedures permitted such disabling under some circumstances"[37].*

6.2.2.   The experiment is delayed

The timetable for the experiment was disrupted when the grid controller delayed the shutdown in order to meet demand for power at 14:00. The reactor was operated at half power during this period (of approximately 11 hours). This moved the experiment from the day shift, which had prepared for it, to the night shift, which hadn't.

The operators might have considered re-establishing the Emergency Core Cooling System but that would have involved significant physical effort and would have had to been reversed before the experiment began. It is not clear if they knew how long the delay was expected to be (in fact it was 11 hours). INSAG-7 do not think that the ECCS would have saved the reactor, nor do they think that rules were broken. However, they conclude that *"Blocking the ECCS over this period and permitting operation for a prolonged period with a vital safety system unavailable are indicative of an absence of safety culture"*.

By 00:05 on 26th April the power level had decreased to 720 MWt and continued to be reduced. The reactor operated below 700 MWt which, it seems, was known to the reactor designers to be unsafe. INSAG-1 was of the opinion that operating at below 700 MWt was forbidden but INSAG-7 had a different view.

INSAG-7 tells us that *"the statement made in INSAG-1 (p. 15) that 'continuous operation below 700 MW(t) is forbidden by normal safety procedures owing to problems of thermal-hydraulic instability' was based on oral statements made by Soviet experts during the week following the Vienna meeting. In fact, sustained operation of the reactor at a power level below 700 MW(t) was not proscribed, either in design, in regulatory limitations or in operating instructions. The emphasis placed on this statement in INSAG-1 was not warranted. After the fact, it is clear that such a proscription should have applied'*

This is evidence that the soviet experts knew more about the potential errant behaviour of the reactor and its various instabilities than the reactor operators knew. This is an intolerable situation.

---

[37] This capability exists in most, if not all, nuclear power plants. Careful procedures control the use of such safety system bypass capabilities. INSAG-1 seems to have ignored this fact in its apparent willingness to accept that the operators were to blame.

At reactor thermal power of about 500 MW (at 00:28) a transfer from the local to global main range automatic power control (automatic power controllers Nos 1 and 2) was noted in the log book. During the transfer there was a significant and unexpected reduction in thermal power to 30 MW, which was not envisaged in the testing programme. This caused xenon levels to start to rise (the rate of production from decay of I-135 would be unaffected whereas the loss due to neutron capture would have dropped significantly).

INSAG-7 has "*the INSAG-1 report describes the precipitous fall in power to 30 MW(t) as being due to an operator error. But later reports suggested that there was no operator error as such; the SCSSINP Commission report refers to an 'unknown cause and inability to control the power', and A.S. Dyatlov, former Deputy Chief Engineer for Operations at the Chernobyl plant, in a private communication refers to the system not working properly*'.

The test plan called for the reactor to be stable at 700 - 1000 MWt (compared to design full power of 3,200 MWt) but attempts to increase power were frustrated by a combination of xenon poisoning, reduced coolant void and graphite cooling. Plokhy (Ref. 35) reports that two operators (Leonid Toptunov, the senior engineer[38], and Yuri Trehub, the previous Shift's lead) switched off the automatic control system and manually withdrew rods until the power levels were back to 200 MW$_t$ at which point the automatic system was reengaged. Given the size of the reactor and the lack of local power measurements the operators were working on intuition (guess work might be an equally fair term) when deciding which rods to pull and how far. They only had the total power figure to work to. At this stage more control rods were withdrawn from the reactor than was allowed by the operating rules. The operators may have been unaware of this and unaware of the significance.

At 00:43:27 the turbo-generator trip signal was blocked in accordance with the experiment plan. This signal would have tripped the reactor as soon as the turbines were tripped but that would have only slowed the accident sequence. The earlier INSAG-1 had this blocking occurring earlier and being in breach of operating rules. They highlighted it as a significant contributor to the accident. INSAG-7 changed the timing, admitted that it was done in accordance with the operational procedures and test procedures and withdrew their earlier statement that the trip would have saved the reactor.

At 01:03, the reactor was stabilised at about 200 MWt and it was decided that the test would be carried out at this power level. There was a need to keep pulling rods

---

[38] 25 year old Toptunov had only been in this job for a couple of months.

further out of the reactor to counterbalance Xenon build-up. (See Figure 16) which shows the xenon reactivity rising after the fall to 30MW$_t$).

At 01.03 and 01.07 additional main cooling pumps were engaged on each side of the reactor. These were to keep the reactor cool during and after the run-down of the turbines and pumps involved in the experiment. All eight main coolant pumps were now operating at full flow, an unusual configuration but not one banned by any document. Remember that the experiment design was for the reactor to be at 700 - 1000 MW$_t$ at this stage not 200 MW$_t$. At the low power level the increased coolant flow over-cooled the reactor graphite, decreasing reactivity and causing control rods to move further out to compensate. The pumps may have exceeded their allowed limits.

With poor steam quality (more water, less steam), the level in the steam drums dropped below the first set point and the alarm level was reduced from -600 mm to -1100 mm (this action was permissible).

At 01:06 (INSAG) or 01.19 (approx) (WNA) the operators increased feed water flow (from the turbine condensers to the water side of the steam separators) in an attempt to bring the steam drum level back into normal operational range. This added colder, denser water to the cooling circuit and further reduced reactivity. The automatic control rods reached the upper limit of their travel and manual rods were also raised. To arrest falling pressures a steam bypass valve was closed (this would have been bleeding off a fraction of the steam and passing it directly into the turbine condensers, bypassing the turbines and therefore removing heat from the system) and automatic trip systems based on the drum were deactivated. Steam pressure continued to drop slowly.

6.2.3. We are now ready for an accident

Having dropped the power from 500 MW$_t$ to 30 MW$_t$ and then recovered to 200 MW$_t$ there was an increasing xenon transient absorbing neutrons and causing the control rods to move out to compensate.

There was a double peaked axial power density distribution over most of the core, the neutron flux being higher in the upper part of the core. This was normal for an RBMK at this stage in its fuel cycle with xenon poisoning higher in the central parts of the reactor and the control rods in high positions. It was, however, a very unfavourable situation in combination with the design of the control rods.

At this stage the reactor had a higher than normal flow rate of coolant because eight, rather than six, main coolant pumps were in operation which, combined with low reactor power, resulted in poor steam quality and low coolant voidage. Circuit hydraulic resistance was lower than expected for the experiment (it is easier to pump water than a water/steam mixture). What little boiling there was occurring near the top of the reactor. As a result, sub-cooling of the coolant at the main coolant pumps was as low as 3°C in some channels. The lower portions of the core had solid water in the coolant flow but it was close to the boiling temperature. Steam pressure and water level in the separators was also low. With an unacceptably high number of rods withdrawn the absorption of neutrons in the lower part of the core was now unhealthily dependent on this water. A small power increase (for whatever reason) could result in a larger than usual increase in the volumetric steam quality in the lower part of the core and this could have a large impact on local reactivity. The reactor's positive void coefficient was higher than usual.

If the experiment had been performed at the power level specified the steam quality would have been better and therefore the degree of sub-cooling greater. Had it not been for the unplanned power transient more control rods would have been deeper in the reactor, reducing the positive void coefficient, and the power distribution would not have been so distorted by the xenon poisoning.

At this stage the operators had no indications that the reactor was in a dangerous situation and had no idea that such a dangerous situation was even possible. They had worked hard to raise reactor power after the unexpected drop and worked hard to manage the steam drum levels. Reports suggest that they were tired and stressed.

6.2.4.   The experiment starts (and finishes)

At 01:21:50 the operators reduced the feed water flow rate sharply which caused an increase in the reactor inlet temperature shortly afterwards.

At 01:23:04 the test started. Turbine generator 8's throttle valve was closed isolating it from the reactor. At 01:23:10 the DBA button was pressed. This is a button specially installed for test purposes, the signal was to be transmitted to the start-up circuit of the diesel generator and to the turbo-generator rundown system to start that.

Coolant flow in the reactor slowed as the main coolant pumps connected to the turbine started to run down. Steam pressure rose due to the combined effects of removing the steam load (disconnecting the turbines) and the reduction in feed water rate (operator action). The ensuing increase in the void fraction as water turned to steam in the coolant circuit resulted in an increase in reactivity and a consequent increase in reactor power.

INSAG-7 speculates that the pumping of coolant was affected by more than just the run-down of the pumps. "*There remain questions of whether pumping capability deteriorated further during this period, with pumps circulating a mixed steam-water* mixture, or whether pumps even cavitated and ceased to circulate the coolant" (INSAG-7).

There is also a suggestion (Ref. 32) that the electric motors powering the main cooling pumps were shut down by safety devices monitoring the voltage and current being supplied to them. If this were so then further questions should be asked about the design of the experiment.

Plokhy (Ref. 35) reports that the speed of turbine 8 dropped rapidly as expected and that the generator started up again at the level specified in the test programme. The test lasted thirty-six seconds.

At 01:23:40 an operator pressed the reactor Shut-down button, called EPS-5 or AZ-5 depending on the translation, to inject control rods into the reactor. Due to the design fault in the control rods the initial impact of this was to increase the reactivity at the bottom of the reactor. There is discussion about why the operator pressed the Shut-down button when he did. INSAG-7 has "*The Commission was unable to establish why the button* [AZ-5] *was pressed*". Was it in response to the rapidly rising power density in the reactor or because the experiment was complete and he wanted to shut the reactor down and finish his shift? (Ref. 33).

It is important to understand that the temporary addition of a little reactivity as the leading edge of a single control rod or a few control rods are motored in from the top of a normally operating reactor of this size should not be a problem although it is a bit odd. The neutron population would change too slowly for it to matter. The problem here was the simultaneous injection of a large number of control rods, spread across a reactor that was already on the edge.

The design fault with the control rods was known. INSAG-7 has "*The existence of the positive scram effect was first acknowledged by Soviet experts at the Conference on Nuclear Power Performance and Safety in Vienna in 1987. The SCSSINP Commission report states that this phenomenon had been known of at the time of the accident and that it had first been identified at the Ignalina RBMK plant in the Lithuanian Republic in 1983. Although the Chief Design Engineer for RBMK reactors promulgated this information to other RBMK plants, and stated that design changes would be made to correct the problem, he made no such changes, and the procedural measures he recommended for inclusion in plant operating instructions were not adopted. Apparently, there was a widespread view that the conditions under which the positive scram effect would be important would never occur. However, they did appear in almost every detail in the course of the actions leading to the accident*". This shows a level of complacency that is unacceptable. Procedures and the safety culture try to prevent such complacency the modern nuclear industry.

It is conjectured that the reactor was now being fed, not only with less cooling water but also with warmer cooling water now that the turbines were slowing and the operators had stopped the additional feed to the steam separators. This caused the coolant to boil lower down the reactor than usual and the voids to take longer to clear the reactor. The resulting voids reduced neutron absorption which led to an increase in reactivity and a runaway increase in power.

At 01:23:43 the power, estimated to be 530 MWt at this stage, was continuing to rise (remember that less than a second earlier it had been about 200 MWt). The power excursion rate emergency protection system signals came on but by this time the reactor was beyond recovery.

The control rods did fully insert. Apparently the various official records are inconsistent on how far the rods moved (Ref. 71). INSAG-7 has "*Their positions, recorded for the last time at 01:22:37, were 1.4, 1.6 and 0.2 m for automatic regulators Nos 1, 2 and 3 respectively*". Ref. 72 has "*the end positions of the CPS rods according to synchro transducers showed that about half of the rods had stopped at depths of 3.5 m to 5.5 m*". These suggest that they did not get very far into the reactor. The core height is 7m.

01:23:46 the first pair of main coolant pumps being run down disconnected followed almost immediately by the second pair.

The rapid increase in fuel temperature would have resulted in more resonance absorption of neutrons and would have helped to curtail the power transient. But it was not enough.

6.2.5.   "Severe shocks"

At 01:23:44 the operators heard banging noises. It is postulated that these were the rupturing of pressure tubes as the fuel disintegrated at high temperature and that the damage to the reactor that this caused prevented the control rods moving in.

At 01:23:47 there was a sharp reduction in the flow rates from the MCPs not included in the experiment and unreliable reading from the ones involved in the experiment. There was a sharp increase in the pressure in the steam drums and in the water level in the steam separators.

At 01:23:49 the rupture of fuel channels and the failure of automatic power controllers was signalled.

At 01:23:48 a high pressure failure blew the top of the reactor. Since all the pressure tubes were connected to this the reactor was comprehensively disassembled. Then at

01:24:00 there was a second loud noise reported by the Control Room and hot fragments were blown out of the Reactor Hall causing fires over a wide area.

At 01:24 the chief reactor control engineer noted in his operating log: "*Severe shocks; the RCPS rods stopped moving before they reached the lower limit stop switches; power switch of clutch mechanisms is off.*"

A generally accepted explanation of these observations is that with the rapid rise in neutron density matched by an equally rapid rise in heat generation within the fuel pins, the insides of the fuel pins heated rapidly and expanded. The pins exploded sending very hot particles into the coolant water which flashed off to steam, blew off the channel plugs and displaced the 2,500 Tonne roof slab[39]. This first explosion would have ruptured all of the pressure tubes since they were connected to the roof slab. Their destruction and the steam pressure resulting from the release of the water in the coolant channels onto the hot graphite fired the roof slab 10 - 14 m into the air. Its fall back into the reactor causing further damage.

The second explosion is ascribed to a chemical explosion resulting from the generation of explosive gases from the fuel-water and water-graphite contact or to a local prompt criticality that saw the reactor power output soar producing a mini nuclear explosion. The former explanation was suggested by the soviet experts at the Post-Accident Review Meeting in Vienna (Ref. 29). The second suggestion came later.

Burning graphite and hot fuel were ejected from the building and were reported to have started approximately 30 fires on the surrounding buildings, including the Turbine Hall shared with Reactor 3.

6.2.6.   INSAG-7 summary

INSAG-7 states that "*Most analyses now associate the severity of the accident with the defects in the design of control and safety rods in conjunction with the physics design characteristics, which permitted the inadvertent setting up of large positive void coefficients. The scram just before the sharp rise in power that destroyed the reactor may well have been the decisive contributory factor.*

On the other hand, the features of the RBMK reactor had also set other pitfalls for the operating staff. Any of these could just as well have caused the initiating event for this or an almost identical accident. They included:

— Pump failure, disturbance of the function of coolant pumping or pump cavitation,

---

[39] It is noted in Ref. 73 that when the fuel reached its melting point the energy used to melt it would not raise its temperature. Similarly with the evaporation phase. The temperature of the fuel would not be rising so the Resonance Absorption would not be increasing further.

combined with the effect of the positive void coefficient. Any of these causes could have led to sudden augmentation of the effect of the positive void coefficient.

— Failure of zirconium alloy fuel channels or of the welds between these and the stainless steel piping, most probably near the core inlet at the bottom of the reactor. Failure of a fuel channel would have been a cause of a sudden local increase in void fraction as the coolant flashed to steam; this would have led to a local reactivity increase which could have triggered a propagating reactivity effect."

6.2.7. A picture worthy of the pen of the great Dante

Plokhi (Ref. 35), Leatherbarrow (Ref. 36), Medvedev (Ref. 37) and Imanaka (Ref. 74) all report eye witness reports and reactions on site and from Moscow and Kiev in the immediate aftermath of the accident. These have been dramatized by Sky and HBO (Ref. 75).

Eyewitnesses report seeing the reactor top "shaking and bending", "violent shudders" from the main circulating pumps. A nearby worker is quoted as hearing a "*loud clap*" and then "*something like the sound of an explosion. I thought it was the steam valve, which we hear from time to time. Then in a couple of seconds a bright, blue flash was followed by an enormous explosion. When looking at Block 4, I saw that there were only two walls left. The structure was in ruins, water was pouring out, bitumen was burning on the roof of Unit 4*'.

There were a number of fishermen in the area. The site's cooling ponds were well stocked with fish and fishing was a popular pastime. (There were a lot of fish in the cooling waters when I was there in 2011, see photo Figure 22). It is reported (by Plokhy (Ref. 35) and by Mahaffy (Ref. 34) that the fishermen continued to fish unperturbed by the explosions but later suffered acute radiation syndrome, which they survived.

In the control room they heard a roaring sound "*that roar was of a completely unfamiliar kind, very low in tone, like a human moan*" (Razim Davletbaev quoted by Plokhy (Ref. 35). Trehub (same reference) remembered it "*But not as an earthquake, if you counted ten seconds, there came a roar, and the frequency of the shocks diminished but their strength increased. Then came the sound of the blast*".

"*The floor and the wall shook violently, dust and bits of debris fell from the ceiling, the luminescent lighting went off, semi-darkness descended, and only the emergency lighting was on*" (Davletbaev quoted in Plokhy (Ref. 35)).

The operators tried to make sense of the explosions they had felt and heard and of the readings on their control panels. The indicators on the control panel were not shedding much light on the issue. They were either dead or showing hard to understand values. We, of course, now know that this was because the detector heads feeding the dials, like the reactor they were monitoring, had already been comprehensively destroyed.

Plokhy (Ref. 35), Medvedev (Ref. 37) and Higginbotham (Ref. 38) all describe the actions taken by those in the control room, those out on site, the fire service and the site management based on testimony and interviews. They paint a picture of desperate people struggling to comprehend what had happened and making vain attempts to save a reactor that was already destroyed. There were many acts of individual and collective bravery. Some of the honours granted to those who worked at Chernobyl can be found in the President of Ukraine Decree № 1156/2008 (which can be translated from Ref. 77). Fifteen of these awards were posthumous.

Diatlov is reported as describing the scene in the turbine hall as "*a picture worthy of the pen of the great Dante. Streams of hot water were bursting in every direction from the damaged pipes and falling on the electrical equipment*". He ordered electrical isolations to be made where possible and for reactor 3 to be shut down. He also ordered all those who were not essential to leave the area, concerned about the levels of radiation.

Meanwhile, the station fire service had responded to the explosions and alarms. On seeing the situation they had declared the highest level of alert available to them to summon support from the entire Kiev region.

On the roof of the turbine hall the firefighters tried to contain the spread of fire to protect the valuable equipment contained in the hall. They report kicking aside "*luminous, silvery pieces of debris of some kind ... one moment they just seemed to lie there, the next moment they would catch fire*" (Shavrei, fireman quoted in Plokhy (Ref. 35)). These were highly radioactive pieces of graphite and nuclear fuel.

Chernobyl's manager Viktor Briukhanov, was alerted and made his way to site. On seeing the top of Unit 4 missing he called in all of the site managers and ordered the emergency bunker to be opened (Figure 23). The first brief to him apparently reported that a hydrogen build-up had caused an explosion in an emergency water tank, but the reactor was intact (Ref. 36). Radiation levels were reported to be high but not nearly as high as they actually were. A difficultly encountered was that the radiation levels were off-scale for almost all of the detectors on site[40].

---

[40] Some radiation detectors will show a full scale deflection (maximum dose reading) when exposed to higher radiation levels than their operating range. Others will show zero as their internal electronics switch off to protect themselves. Those trained to use radiation monitoring devices should understand this and be wary if they see full scale deflections or zero when they are not expected.

Figure 22 Fish in the cooling waters at Chernobyl (Photo K.I.Pearce)

Within the bunker control room an initial report on the accident was prepared. This underestimated the extent of the damage to the reactor and the dose levels in the area. Evacuation of the surrounding area was discussed between the site manager and local Communist Party Officials and it was agreed not to recommend that. There seems to have been a real reticence to make the big decisions. Instead people played for time hoping that a more senior person would arrive and take responsibility. Over reacting, or even promulgating bad news, was feared to be career limiting.

It is reported (Ref. 35) that Mikhail Gorbachev, the general secretary of the Communist Party of the Soviet Union (the leader of the Union), was informed of the accident at about 5 am on April 26th (four hours after the first explosion). He was told of explosions and fires but reassured that the reactor was intact. A state commission was initiated to examine the causes of the accident and to deal with its consequences. High powered members of this commission started to leave Moscow around 9 a.m to fly to Kiev and travel to the site from there.

The initial thoughts of those off-site seemed to be concentrated on how the reactor could be repaired and restarted and even when the commission arrived on site and saw the extent of the damage they were slow to accept the severity of the accident.

Apparently it was not until later when two experts from Moscow flew a helicopter over the reactor with a photographer that the commission had to accept that the reactor would not be back on the power grid anytime soon, in fact the reactor no longer existed. Judging by the descriptions of the colour of the core reported by different people at different times it was getting hotter.

It was after 11 p.m. that the decision was finally made to evacuate the population. The announcement to the public can be heard in Ref. 2 (at time 6.01). This evacuation began in earnest in the early afternoon of April 27th, a day and a half after the initial explosions. It was undertaken efficiently and effectively.

It took several weeks to bring the situation under control (Ref. 28) in which time about 1800 helicopter trips dropped about 5000t of materials into the reactor area to absorb neutrons (boron carbide), smother the fire (dolomite), provide filtration (sand and clay) and provide a heat sink (lead). This improvisation was not totally successful, causing some additional damage and possibly providing insulation to make the temperature rise higher. It is, however, hard to state with any confidence how different the outcome would have been if other approaches had been taken.

The addition of cooling water was stopped as it was not particularly successful and was endangering other units with flooding. Liquid nitrogen was poured into the area to provide cooling and to provide an inert layer to reduce oxidation.

A tunnel was dug below the reactor and filled with concrete and a cooling system.

By the end of November that year a shelter had been built over the damaged reactor building in an attempt to prevent further release of activity. This was largely an improvised structure made under extremely trying circumstances; building over a badly damaged and unstable reactor building and in areas with very high radiation dose. See Wikipedia *Chernobyl Nuclear Power Plant sarcophagus* (Ref. 78). This has since been enclosed in the Chernobyl New Safe Confinement, the result of a major engineering project (Ref. 79 and 80).

6.3. Blame

Fourteen months after the accident, six of the Chernobyl staff were tried in a temporary court room of the Culture Centre in the nearby evacuated town of Chernobyl. Apparently it was necessary under soviet law to try people near to the scene of the alleged crime.

Figure 23 Strategic Management Room of Chernobyl Emergency Control Bunker (Photo K.I.Pearce)

Formally it was an "open trial" and journalists were present for at least some of the sessions but it was within the 30 km exclusion zone. The trial lasted 18 days from the 7th to the 29th of July 1987. I have been unable to find anything approaching an official record of the event. A short account of the trials can be found in Ref. 81.

The Site Director, Viktor Briukhanov, was expelled from the Communist Party in July 1986 "*for major errors and shortcomings in work leading to an accident with serious consequences*" prior to his arrest. He was then charged with breach of safety rules at enterprises subject to explosive hazards; abuse of power; and with negligence. He was found guilty and sentenced to 10 years in a labour camp.

Nikolai Fomin, the site's Chief Engineer, and Anatolii Diatlov, his deputy, who was in the Control Room during the accident received the same punishment.

The three other defendants were: Oleksii Kovalenko, chief of the reactor division on site; Boris Rogozhkin, the chief of the plant's shift on the night of the accident; and Yurii Laushkin, an official of the nuclear safety commission. They received sentences of between two to five years in labour camps.

The Soviet system needed someone to blame and it was easy to blame the operators. They closed off safety systems, they pulled out more rods than were sensible, and they pushed the buttons to start the test and then pushed the button to insert the control rods. If they hadn't done all of those things the accident would not have happened. This seems to have been the main theme of INSAG-1, the western world's first in-depth review of the accident.

Nikolai N. Ponomarev-Stepnoi a member of the U.S.S.R. Academy of Sciences and First Deputy Director of the Kurchatov Institute of Atomic Energy is quoted as saying in 1988 *"The causes of the Chernobyl Nuclear Power Plant accident are associated primarily with mistakes made by station personnel, by their violations of established operating procedures for nuclear power plants"*.

He went on to defend nuclear power in the following terms: *"Analysis of the consequences of the Chernobyl accident demonstrates that although the losses due to the accident were significant, they are nonetheless comparable with the losses due to other major industrial and transportation accidents. If nuclear power production sources are replaced by traditional ones, the health risk to the population and risks to the environment may increase"* (Ref. 83).

Placing the blame on the operators was politically expedient as it exonerated the political hierarchy, the nuclear industry as a whole and the reactor design in particular. But it did not stick. It was too superficial.

Another defensive position held in the west is that the experiment was badly designed and badly executed, neither of which could happen here. INSAG-7 (Section 5.2.2) implies that the Russians defended the experiment going ahead at a lower power level than that intended because it was not specifically banned in the test procedure. INSAG conclude that:

"However, the facts are that:

— the test procedure was altered on an ad hoc basis;

— the reason for this was the operators' inability to achieve the prescribed test power level;

— this was the case because of reactor conditions that arose owing to the previous operation at half power and the subsequent reduction to very low power levels;

— as a result, when the test was initiated the disposition of the control rods, the power distribution in the core and the thermal-hydraulic conditions were such as to render the reactor highly unstable".

Some, at least, of the blame belongs to the economic and political systems that put pressure on people to achieve targets while paying lip service to quality and safety. In Ref. 4 Zheludev and Konstantinov, in an address to the IAEA in 1980 (6 years before the accident), state that "*In the Soviet Union, much attention is being paid to ensuring the safety of nuclear power plants. Scientifically sound standards and rules for nuclear and radiation safety in the planning, construction and operation of nuclear power plants have been formulated, and special supervisory bodies for nuclear power plant safety have been established. It may be said with confidence that by taking the proper technical and organizational precautions now we can guarantee the safe development of nuclear power on a large scale*". Those "proper technical and organisational precautions" clearly did not do the job expected of them and their guarantee was worthless.

Grigori Medvedev, an engineer associated with the building of Chernobyl, reports (Ref. 37) that there had been a number of nuclear accidents in the USA and USSR but that none of the nuclear power station accidents in the Soviet Union were publically reported with the exception of a few hints here and there[41]. An unfortunate effect of this silence is that it denies the designers and operators of power plant the opportunity to learn from past events, thus making them more likely to reoccur, and engenders an unwarranted belief in the infallibility of such systems.

In the west there was a readiness to accept the blame aimed at the operators. We have already discussed INSAG-1 and the subsequent partial back peddling in INSAG-7. In addition the reactor design and build quality also came in for strong criticism, not only in INSAG-7. The World Nuclear Association has "*The Chernobyl accident in 1986 was the result of a flawed reactor design that was operated with inadequately trained personnel*" (Ref. 84). See also Hansard House of Commons debate 24 March 1987 which reports that "*Vastly larger numbers of people have died from accidents due to fire in the last few years than from accidents due to nuclear power generation, including Chernobyl, which would not and could not have happened here*" (Lord James Douglas-Hamilton) (Ref. 85).

Again, placing the blame on foreign operators operating foreign designed and built reactors protected the western world's nuclear industry. If that failed, the next line of defence, was to admit that the nuclear industry does kill people but not as many as other industries.

INSAG-7 holds the view that the experiment should have been abandoned when the specified initial conditions could not have been reached. Wise words with the benefit of hind sight.

INSAG-7 does make many corrections to INSAG-1 where blame had been put on the operators. A more measured review shows that a lot of the steps that INSAG-1

---

[41] If you are interested to read about nuclear accidents the IAEA compilation (Ref. 86) is a good place to start. (Ref. 34) is also a good read.

claimed were counter to the rules were not at all and that some of the inherent dangers of the reactor design were known but had not been adequately communicated to the operators.

So, who or what is to blame for the Chernobyl accident?

The fact is that there were many opportunities to prevent the Chernobyl accident including better design of plant, better build quality, a real desire to learn from experience[42], an atmosphere where questions are permitted and concerns listened to and acted upon, more awareness in managers, experiment designers and operators. The world was unlucky that fate found a way through all the safety barriers at the same time on 26th April 1986 but, to a certain extent, you make your luck.

I believe that it is telling that the RBMK reactors were reviewed and a number of safety related changes made to the whole fleet.

7. Other suggested explanations of the accident

There is still some doubt about the exact causes of the explosions experienced at Chernobyl and it is probably that the truth will never been known for sure. Some of the doubts result from the original deliberate obscuration by the Soviets and there are some oddball theories but there is also room to question the nature of the explosions that wrecked the reactors.

See for example Reference 70 which is from a web-site written by a Russian Reactor Physicist who has some highly individualistic views on the reactor design, the accident and the investigation. To quote his web-site "*All scientific and technical investigations of the causes of the Chernobyl accident which have been carried out throughout the past 20 years, are nonsensical, false or erroneous. The initial information about the accident is inaccurate, garbled, counterfeited and was partially destroyed by operational personnel immediately after the emergency. And even experts themselves are not to be believed, since half of them were operational personnel, who would do anything to protect corporate interests*". I'm not entirely sure what to make of the site, it should probably be treated with healthy scepticism.

---

[42] High risk industries use many different techniques to minimise accidents and to learn as much as possible from accidents and near misses that do occur. One of these is "root cause analysis" which forces you review the situation in a highly structured manner. One aspect is to keep asking why and drilling deeper. See, for example, Ref. 34 for an overview of the technique and Ref. 35 for a detailed manual for its use within the nuclear industry.

Slightly more credible are the two articles by the plant's former deputy chief engineer responding to some criticism of the Chernobyl crew (Refs. 30 and 31) and suggesting that the design of the reactor was more important than the operators' actions in the accident. His testimony cannot be considered to be entirely disinterested. He was a successful plant manager until, blamed for his role in the accident, he was sentenced to ten years in a labour camp but released after five because the radiation dose he received in the aftermath had damaged his health.

INSAG-7 listed thirteen possible explanations for the rapid increase in reactivity.

The officially favoured version is that a power surge at the bottom of the reactor caused some of the fuel to overheat and rupture. This destroyed the pressure tubes leading to the contact of water and hot graphite which caused the first explosion; a steam expansion explosion. Subsequent explosions were then the ignition of explosive gases produced by the interaction of hot fuel and hot cladding with the steam.

B.I.Gorbachev (Ref. 71) mentions the 1995 suggestion that an earthquake was the cause of the event but this does not seem to have been taken seriously. At least one careful consideration of the possibility dismisses it (Ref. 87).

In 1999 Konstantin Checherov, a physicist from Russia's Kurchatov Institute, published a paper (Ref. 88) in which he claims to have spoken to eye witnesses who are convinced that the first big explosions occurred before the reactor was scrammed. He believes that four of the Main Cooling Pumps were shut down by the circuits monitoring the state of health of their electrical supply causing the coolant flow to stall. This resulted in a sudden increase in voidage and a spike in the power output. He claims that the increase in pressure pushed the reactor, or at least parts of it, into the air before it exploded.

As recently as 2017 another version was suggested. This time by a trio of Swedish physicists (Ref. 89) who suggest that the first explosion was a nuclear power spike in one or a few of the fuel channels and that the second was the steam explosion that is usually identified as the first. They suggest that the nuclear explosions caused a jet of debris that reached an altitude of some 2500 to 3000 m and that this better explains the distribution of some of the fission fragments measured around Europe.

As I said in my introduction, I am not going to express an opinion on the nature of the explosions. The reactor was manoeuvred into a situation where a power surge took place. Two main explosions are reported by witnesses. These could have been physical, chemical or nuclear in nature. I hope I have explained why the power surge happened.

8. Fallout

The site released significant amounts of radioactive material over the next ten days. This varied in chemical and physical form and in the height it reached above the station. All of these parameters affect how the radioactivity interacts with the weather and migrates. It is borne by the wind, spreading out as it goes and is deposited onto the ground. Most of the activity was deposited near to the site but some travelled a significant distance.

There is still some debate about how much radioactivity was released, with a steady stream of papers being published since the accident. For example a new paper on the subject was published as recently as 2017 (Ref. 90).

Deposition of Chernobyl activity was measured over wide areas of Europe, including the UK. Some areas in Cumbria and Scotland were subjected to controls on what could be produced for human consumption and these controls lasted for many years. Controls on sheep meat were finally withdrawn in 2012 (Ref. 91).

A nice graphic from the UK Met. Office that shows the dispersion of activity around Europe can be found as Ref. 92. It is clear that almost everyone in Europe that fortnight will have received an additional radiation dose as a result of the accident. An estimate put this as a 15% increase on the average background dose in the north and 1% in the south (Ref. 93).

There is a wide spread of the estimates of the number of people in Europe killed by the accident exist, see for example Ref. 94. The reason for this is that if the linear no-threshold model of radiation harm is accepted then a radiation dose, no matter how small, has a chance of initiating a cancer that will eventually kill a person. If you add up all the very small chances of a given individual dying over all of the people in the wide area affected by Chernobyl fallout you arrive at a figure of "deaths" that can range up to tens of thousands. These deaths are unlikely to be noticed as Chernobyl related because they will occur decades later and because so many people will die of cancer from other causes, most of which will be unknown, in that time that any extra ones do not show up.

UNSCEAR[43] (Ref. 95) states that 30 workers died within a few weeks of the accident and over a hundred others suffered radiation induced injuries. About 115,000 people were evacuated from the area around the reactor followed by a further 220,000 people from areas of Belarus, the Russian Federation and Ukraine. There was no

---

[43] The United Nations Scientific Committee on the Effects of Atomic Radiation (UNSCEAR), was established by the General Assembly of the United Nations in 1955. Its mandate in the United Nations system is to assess and report levels and effects of exposure to ionizing radiation.

evidence of a major public health impact attributable to radiation in the twenty years after the accident except for a significant increase in child thyroid cancers, more than 6000 cases by 2002.

Average effective doses to those persons most affected by the accident were assessed to be about 120 mSv for 530,000 recovery operation workers, 30 mSv for 115,000 evacuated persons and 9 mSv during the first two decades after the accident to those who continued to reside in contaminated areas. By comparison the average annual background dose in the UK is about 2.7 mSv (Ref. 96 and Figure 24) and radiation worker dose limits are 20 mSv a year with limits of 50 mSv a year for special cases (Ref. 97).

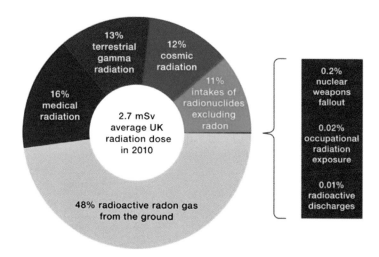

Figure 24 Background radiation in the UK (From PHE)

9. What is keeping us safe?

A frequently asked question is "is nuclear power safe?" This is a very vague question as the word "safe" has a range of meaning. It is not the question this book set out to discuss. The nuclear industry is not immune to accidents, many have been recorded (Ref. 86) including, the well-known ones, Windscale, Three Mile Island, Chernobyl and Fukushima. On the other hand, relatively few people have been killed or had their health damaged as a result of the nuclear industry and it provides copious amounts of electricity without burning fossil fuels.

The Chernobyl accident, as we have seen, happened against a background of a society driven by unrealistic targets that were routinely missed or fudged. Of these the latter is probably the most alarming. Equipment intended for installation in nuclear power plants was often delivered in a condition unfit to use. Within this system people at all levels were bullied to achieve arbitrary targets. Failure often meant humiliation in front of your peers or loss of standing and access to the comfortable life achieved by some.

Another aspect of this was the lack of openness. Accidents happened at nuclear and non-nuclear plant but news of them did not travel. An important part of the current "safety culture" is a process given many names including "operational feedback". In this system accidents and near-misses are carefully reported and analysed and any lessons communicated to those that might benefit from the knowledge including plant managers, team leaders and reactor operators (Ref. 98 - 99).   Maybe with this system the Chernobyl reactor would have had better designed control rods, the operators may have been more aware that too many rods had been removed and better understood the impact of that on plant safety. Maybe, without the belief in invulnerability that comes from never hearing about problems, the experiment would have been postponed.

The impression is given that, prior to the Chernobyl accident, the Russian regulators seemed more concerned with increasing output and finding people to blame and punish if targets were not kept than in ensuring safe operation. By contrast the nuclear regulators[44] in most, if not all, other countries are not concerned with production and profits but are focussed upon safe design, construction, maintenance and operation of nuclear sites. They are independent and should not be influenced by either industry or government.

Following the accident at Chernobyl on 26th April 1986 the World Association of Nuclear Operators (WANO) was founded in 1989. The WANO mission is "*to maximise the safety and reliability of nuclear power plants worldwide by working together to assess, benchmark and improve performance through mutual support, exchange of information, and emulation of best practice*"[45].

Through the WANO programme of peer reviews, Significant Operating Experience Reports (SOERs), Significant Event Reports (SERs) and technical support & exchange, members can learn from the experiences of other operators. The willingness of

---

[44] See for example
Nuclear Regulatory Commission (US NRC) in the United States of America - https://www.nrc.gov/
The Office for Nuclear Regulation (ONR) in the UK http://www.onr.org.uk/
Nuclear Safety Authority (ASN) in France http://www.french-nuclear-safety.fr/

[45] I have been on WANO peer review (Ref. 100) visits to Phillipsburg NPP in Germany and Kozloduy NPP, Bulgaria. I wonder how many other industries make it possible for team-leaders from one country to challenge Site Directors, town mayors, reactor operators and emergency responders about the safety of their plant and their ability to respond to emergencies.

WANO members to openly share their operating experience for the benefit of other nuclear operators is fundamental to the success of this programme (Ref. 101).

The nuclear industry talks about defence in depth (see, for example Ref. 102), multiple layers of protection and the Swiss cheese model of accident prevention (Ref. 103). They all boil down to having multiple independent layers. This is illustrated in Figure 25 (From IAEA, INSAG-12, Ref. 102) which shows a series of physical barriers and levels of protection considering these to be like a series of obstacles protecting the public and environment from harm from the radioactive material in its normal state. To have an accident all of the layers of protection have to be breached at the same time.

A good example of openness and learning from experience is the report produced by the Office for Nuclear Regulation (ONR) in the UK which outlines the events that took place between 2017 and 2017. These reports are "*designed to give people confidence in how nuclear sites are regulated on the rare occasions that safety-significant events occur*" (Ref. 104).

Reactor design has improved significantly driven by challenging targets to make accidental releases far less likely and of much lower consequence. Materials are better and their behaviour in radiation fields and at high temperatures are better understood. Control systems are better; more parameters are measured more often and software systems keep operators informed of key parameters and parameters moving out of their permitted range.

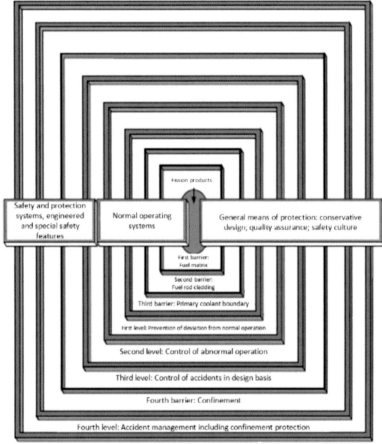

Figure 25 IAEA view of defence in depth

Appendix A - Additional Physics

This Appendix has been added because the description of the Chernobyl accident has required some physics to be explained and some to be taken on trust. This section expands on the atomic and nuclear physics surrounding nuclear reactor physics.

A.1. The atomic model

An aside into quantum weirdness. This section is not vital to the understanding of the Chernobyl accident but introduces some elements of quantum theory which deepens the understanding of atomic and nuclear models.

When it was first proposed the "Rutherford model" of electrons orbiting a massive nucleus caused problems for physicists as, given the physics understanding of the time, it should be unstable. In classical physics any charged particle that is subject to an acceleration, such as an orbiting particle, radiates energy. If this were the case the orbiting electron would give off energy and its orbit would decay. Eventually it would crash into the nucleus.

Prior to 1885 in was known that chemicals could absorb or emit light at very precise wavelengths characteristic of the element. In 1888 Rydberg generalised work performed by Balmer and showed that the wavelength of these lines fitted the equation:

$$\frac{1}{\lambda} = R_H \left(\frac{1}{n_1^2} - \frac{1}{n_2^2} \right)$$

Where

λ is the wavelength of the spectral line (cm)

R_H is the Rydberg constant and is equal to 109,737 cm^{-1}

n_1 and n_2 are integers with $n_2 > n_1$

See Ref. 105 for a nice description.

In 1913 Bohr proposed a model of the atom in which electrons orbited the charged and massive nucleus but only at certain discrete distances from the nucleus in which the electron, for some unknown reason, did not emit electromagnetic radiation. It was proposed that the electron could jump from stationary orbit to stationary orbit absorbing or emitting energy equal to the energy different in the orbits. It was also shown that, if the angular momentum of the electron was given by nh/2π, where h is the Planck constant (6.626 070 15 × 10^{-34} joule-seconds) and n is an integer, then this predicted the spectral lines seen by experimentalist and described by the Rydberg equation (Ref. 112).

We now need to detour into two other areas where classical physics is shown to be wanting; the photoelectric effect and black body radiation.

By the end of the nineteenth century it was known that if you shone light at a metal surface then, under some circumstances, electrons would be emitted. This is the photoelectric effect. The obvious explanation, given the physics of the day in which light was seen as a transverse electromagnetic wave, was that the light waves were acting on the electrons making them vibrate and that every now and again one would get enough energy to escape from the metal. In this model you would expect that bright light would give the electrons more energy.

However, closer investigation (See Lenard's work Ref. 106) showed that the electron's energy was independent of the brightness of the light, that very dim light would produce electrons immediately and that the energy of the electrons depended on the colour of the light. This could not be explained by the physics of the day.

Black body radiation was another mystery. A black body is an ideal radiator - a body that emits as much heat as is theoretically possible given its temperature. The classical treatment of this phenomena leads to the Rayleigh-Jeans equation which fits experimental data at long wavelengths (low energy) but predicts far too much energy emission at small wavelengths (high energy) - the Ultraviolet Catastrophe (Ref. 107). In 1900 Max Planck had shown that the light emitted by such hot bodies could be explained provided that electromagnetic energy could be only emitted in discrete amounts, it is "quantized".

He gave us the equation: $E = h\nu$

Where:

>E is the energy of the photon (J)
>h is the Planck constant is $6.626\ 070\ 15 \times 10^{-34}$ J.s
>ν is the frequency of the radiation (s^{-1})

In 1905 Einstein observed that the photoelectric effect could be explained if the Planck equation was applied to the incident light and that it was considered to be composed of tiny packets of energy; quanta or photons, with the energy of each particle proportional to the frequency of the electromagnetic radiation. Since that time we have had to try to understand that some experiments, such as diffraction, polarization and interference clearly show light to be a wave and not a particle while others, such as the photoelectric effect, equally clearly show it to be composed of particles and not waves. Wave particle duality had arrived (Ref. 108).

In 1924 a French physicist de Broglie argued that if things we thought of as waves had particle properties then maybe things we think of as particles could have wave properties. He deduced the equation:

λ = h/mv where

Where

> λ is the wavelength of the particle (m)
> h is the Planck constant is 6.626 070 15 x 10^{-34} J.s
> m is the mass of the particle (kg)
> v is the velocity of the particle (m.s^{-2})

(Note J has dimensions kg.m^2.s^{-2})

(A translation of his PhD thesis, which contains this work, can be found at Ref. 109)

It is postulated that for an electron orbit to be stable the orbital path length (the circumference of the orbital circuit) has to be a whole number of wavelengths: $2\pi r$ = $n\lambda$ where λ = h/mv (de Broglie). λ is the wavelength of the electron and n is a positive integer (1, 2, 3, 4 ....).

Combining this with the equation of the energy of an orbiting electron KE = $\frac{1}{2}mv^2$ and PE = kq_1q_2/r and you can prove that mvr = $nh/2\pi$. Where k is Coulomb's law constant (approximately 9 x 10^9 N. m^2 / C^2 in air), m is the mass of the electron and v its orbital velocity.

This quantises angular momentum, gives a series of allowed electron orbits and predicts the energy differences between the orbits that can be measured experimentally.

The transition of electrons between the energy levels gives out, or absorbs, a spectrum of photons with discrete energies. The agreement of the predictions of the Rydberg equation with observation is strong evidence of the quantum nature of atoms and nuclei.

Since then quantum mechanics has established itself as a methodology that accurately predicts a wide range of sub-atomic behaviour, including atomic energy spectra. However, trying to understand what quantum mechanics actually means physically is baffling. It describes quantum objects as wave like entities that can be described by a "wave function" which evolves smoothly with time. This wave function is related to the probability of where the particle is and its properties and can suggest that the particle has a number of simultaneous options about these. It is only when a "measurement" is made that one of the possibilities is chosen somehow and the wave function collapses (all the other possibilities go away). Schrodinger's cat (1935) (Ref. 110) is a famous description of the conceptual problems this gives for people living in the "real world" of experience.

In Schrodinger's model of the atom the nucleus is surrounded by a cloud of electron density which give the probability that an electron will be found there if you go and look. The cloud is densest in certain regions which we call the electron orbits or shells. These can be related to Bohr's orbitals.

A.2. Nuclear stability and radioactive decay

A great deal of data has been collected about stable and unstable isotopes. This includes the mass of the nucleus, the half-life of unstable nuclei and how they decay along with more esoteric properties such as energy levels, spin and isospin. The science of nuclear structure seeks to understand this data set in terms of models of the nucleus.

Figure 26 summarises the half-lives of known isotopes in a plot that shows the number of neutrons (x-axis) and the number of protons (y-axis). It shows stable isotopes (shown by black boxes) following the line N = Z at low mass leaning towards a higher ratio of neutrons at higher masses. For helium-4 (2 protons and 2 neutrons) and oxygen-16 (8 protons and 8 neutrons) this ratio is unity. For indium-115 (49 protons and 66 neutrons) the ratio of neutrons to protons has increased to 1.35, and for uranium-238 (92 protons and 146 neutrons) the neutron to-proton ratio is 1.59.

Above z = 92 there are no stable isotopes. There are about 250 stable nuclides. This type of plot is commonly known as the Segre chart they can be used to organise and present a great deal of information. (See Ref. 41).

This shape is sometimes described as showing the "valley of stability" (Ref. 111). If you look along a line of constant z, i.e. at all the isotopes of a given chemical you find stable isotopes in the middle with increasingly unstable (shorter half-live or reduced mass excess shown by lighter coloured boxed) isotopes as you move outwards in either direction.

A lot of research has been undertaken looking at how the nucleus is formed and how it holds together. The keys factors are a *strong force* which pulls the nucleons together and the electrostatic repulsion (Coulomb force) between the charges on the protons. The main properties of the strong nuclear force are:
- It is powerfully repulsive at its core.
- It is strongly attractive at typical nucleon separation distances (1.3×10^{-15}m).
- It is short-ranged, dropping to near zero between 2 and 2.5×10^{-15} m.

The Coulomb force between the charges falls as the square of the distance between them and is significantly weaker than the strong force at ranges where the strong force operates. However, it has a longer range and dominates beyond about 2.5×10^{-15} m.

The strong nuclear force is not connected with charge. The Proton-proton, proton-neutron and neutron-neutron strong force is the same. (The force between protons, however, is modified by the Coulomb repulsion between them.)

Nuclear stability can be seen to be a battle between the attractive strong force and the repulsive Coulomb force (with a few complicating factors described by quantum mechanics thrown in).

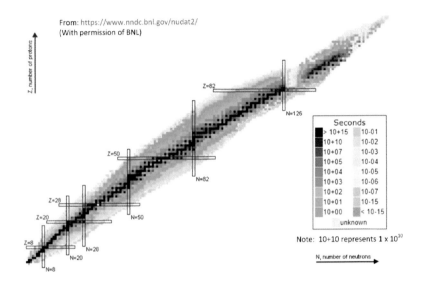

Figure 26 Segre chart showing half-life as a function of N & Z

We can now attempt to understand why the stable region bends from the N=Z line to a higher ratio of neutrons at high mass by observing that the neutrons contribute to the binding offered by the strong nuclear force, as do protons, but, unlike neutrons, protons also add to the repulsive Coulomb force. As the nucleus becomes bigger than the strong nuclear force range and gets more protons, the forces pulling the protons apart exceeds the forces holding them together. At this point the nucleus can accommodate more neutrons but not more protons.

A.3. Beta decay

Moving to the right of the valley of stability (adding neutrons) reaches isotopes with more neutrons than is ideal. These decay either by neutron emission (rare, particularly near the bottom of the valley) or by beta decay (much more common).

Beta decay is a process in which a neutron within a nucleus changes into a proton and spits out an electron (in this circumstance called a "beta particle" or a beta-minus particle) and an anti-neutrino. A mirror process can also occur in which a proton in a proton rich nucleus (left of the valley of stability) decays into a neutron plus a positron (like an electron but with positive charge) and a neutrino.

Example. Beta decay of tritium

$$^{3}_{1}H \rightarrow {}^{3}_{2}He + {}^{0}_{-1}e + {}^{0}_{0}\bar{v}$$

Where

$^{0}_{-1}e$ denotes a beta particle - often shown simply as β

$^{0}_{0}\bar{v}$ denotes an electron anti-neutrino often not shown in this context.

The neutrino and anti-neutrino are ghostly particles, originally postulated to explain why beta decay produced a range of beta energies up to a maximum and seemed to defy the laws of conservation of energy and momentum. With no charge and almost no mass they are very difficult to detect despite being thought to be the most abundant particle in the universe (Ref. 112).

Beta and beta-plus decay change the chemical element concerned (Z is varied by +1 in beta decay and -1 in beta-plus decay). There is no change in the mass number. Decay moves the nucleus nearer to the valley of stability but can lead to it being in an excited state. This excited state will decay to the ground state by giving out a gamma photon or series of photons.

This is shown in Figure 27 for the decay of ^{60}Co to ^{60}Ni. The decay diagram shows two possible beta decays with one much more probable than the other. These both lead to excited states in ^{60}Ni which result in gamma decays as the nucleus transitions to its ground state. Thus, from ^{60}Co we would expect to see a continuum of beta energies up to 1.48 MeV but mainly below 0.31 MeV and two gamma lines at 1.732 MeV and 1.3325 MeV. The lower left inset shows the gamma energy spectrum measured on a NaI detector and the two gamma lines can be clearly seen. The upper right inset shows how the decay moves towards the valley of stability (blue boxes) on the serge chart.

The equation for this decay is:

$$^{60}_{27}Co \longrightarrow {}^{60}_{28}Ni + {}^{0}_{-1}\beta + \bar{v}_e \qquad \text{Where } \bar{v}e \text{ is the electron antineutrino.}$$

Beta decay is clearly proof that the neutron is not a structure less billiard-ball type entity and that the nucleus cannot always be thought of as some kind of bag full of

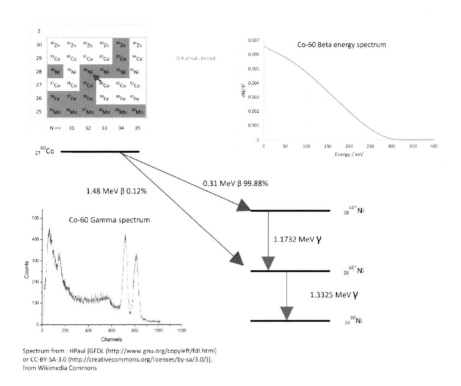

Figure 27 Co-60 decay

red balls (protons) and blue balls (neutrons) despite that fact that this is how it is often drawn.

Beta decay can be "explained" with a knowledge of sub-nucleon structure. Nucleons are composed of particles called "quarks" which come in a six "flavours", Up, Down, Charm, Strange, Top and Bottom. A neutron is composed of 2 down and 1 up whereas a proton is composed of 2 up and 1 down. An aspect of quantum weirdness is that a down quark can spend some time (a very short amount of time ~10^{26}s) as an up quark and a W⁻ boson (W-minus boson). Normally the W⁻ is quickly reabsorbed so nothing has changed. However, if it is energetically favourable, the W⁻ can sometimes decay to give an electron and an anti-neutrino, which head off in different directions, leading to beta decay.

Further reading. See, for example references 112 - 117.

A.4. Alpha decay

Another important decay mode for radioactive nuclei is "alpha decay" in which an unstable nucleus spits out an alpha particle (2 neutrons and 2 protons bound together as a 4-Helium nucleus) and decays to a lighter nucleus (mass number reduced by 4, proton and neutron numbers each reduced by 2). The alpha particle is the most stable nucleus as measured by its binding energy (See later). An example of alpha decay is that of 219-Radon as given below:

$$_{86}^{219}Rn \longrightarrow \; _{84}^{215}Po + \; _{2}^{4}He$$

Or $\qquad _{86}^{219}Rn \longrightarrow \; _{84}^{215}Po + \alpha$ (Different notation)

Alpha decay is a property of heavy nuclei (for light nuclei where binding energy is increasing with increasing mass it is not energetically favourable). With the exception of 8-Berillium which can decay to 2 alpha particles, nothing below Tellurium (Z = 52) has a measurable alpha decay mode.

Alpha particles have a typical kinetic energy of 5 MeV on ejection.

Interestingly, if you happen to like that sort of thing, the observed energies of alpha particles and half-lives of alpha decay could not be explained until the concepts of quantum mechanics were bought to bear on the issue. It is now readily modelled as a quantum tunnelling effect.

Further reading references 118 - 119.

A.5. Spontaneous fission

For some heavy nuclei (approximately 230-Thorium and above) it is energetically favourable to split into two approximately equal "fission fragments" or "fission fragments", which are lighter nuclei, with the release of a few spare neutrons. This is "*spontaneous fission*"

Spontaneous fission half-lives can be very long (for example for ^{238}U the fission half-life is about 10^{16} years) and competes with alpha-decay.

For 235-Uranium a possible spontaneous fission process is:

$$_{92}^{235}U \longrightarrow \; _{54}^{140}Xe + \; _{38}^{92}Sr + 3\,_{0}^{1}n$$

Most fission fragments are radioactive and decay via beta decay. This is because they are neutron rich as they have approximately the same neutron to proton ratio as the heavier elements. This high neutron-to-proton ratio places the fragments below and to the right of the stability curve i.e. in the beta active area.

A.6. Radioactive decay and the Segre Chart

The radioactive decay modes described above all lead to nuclei that are more stable than the parent nuclei. Thus neutron over-rich nuclei decay by beta decay, proton over-rich nuclei decay by beta-plus decay and heavy nuclei either fission or alpha decay.

This is shown very clearly on the Segre chart (Figure 28) where the boxes have been colour coded to signify the principle mode of decay of the nucleus they represent. The black squares represent stable nuclides. Moving right from this line adds progressively more neutrons and takes us away from the line of stability. Out here isotopes want to reduce their ratio of neutrons to protons and they generally do this by **beta decay** which involves the spitting out of a beta particle (electron) and a neutrino (a sub atomic particle that we need not concern ourselves with here) both with some kinetic energy. In the process a sub-atomic neutron is turned into a proton (to understand this we would need to go deeper into the composition of the sub-atomic particles - see reference 120 for more detail).

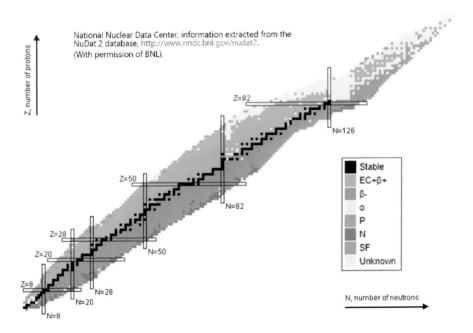

Figure 28 nuclear decay modes on Segre chart

It will be noticed that the black squares in Figure 28 do not go above [209]Bi (Bismuth 209). This is the point where the nucleus is too big to hold together. In these larger nuclei the protons can all feel the repulsion from each other but not the attraction to nucleons on the other side of the nucleus. It becomes unstable. These massive nuclei have a number of different decay modes open to them; the important ones being:

- They can undergo beta decay as described above;

- They can spit out an alpha particle ($^4_2$He) with some kinetic energy producing a lighter less energetic nucleus. This "daughter" nuclide may be stable or may still be unstable and decay again;
- They can undergo **spontaneous fission** in which they split into two or more smaller nuclei.

A.7. Decay chains

When a radioactive nucleus decays in transmutes to a more stable nucleus but it is not always true that the nucleus produced (sometimes called the "daughter" nucleus) is, itself, stable. Multiple decays are possible. These are termed "decay chains" in the literature. See reference 121 for clear pictures of the four main decay chains from actinides.

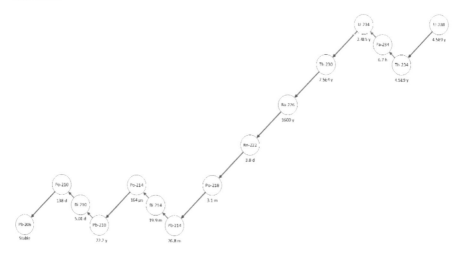

Figure 29 Decay chain of Uranium-238

After each U-235 fission the neutron-rich fission fragments must undergo an average of 6 beta decays to reach stability. These decays are an importance source of decay heat.

A.8. Conservation within radioactive decay

The radioactive decays discussed here result in significant changes within the atomic nucleus but conserve:

- Electric charge. Charges can be neutralised or separated but the overall charge does not change;

- Mass number. The number of nucleons does not change. However, the conversion of a proton to a neutron and vice versa is allowed.
- Mass and energy. Mass can be converted to energy and energy can be converted to mass, but the sum of mass and energy must be constant.
- Momentum. Momentum is conserved. This is responsible for the distribution of the available kinetic energy among product nuclei, particles, and/or radiation.

These rules, particularly the first two, are useful to remember when trying to determine if a particular reaction is allowed.

A.9. Summary of radionuclide decay

Not all combinations of neutron and proton make stable nuclei. In fact stable combinations are quite rare (~250 stable nuclei out of, say, 92^2 (8464) possible combinations ~ 3%).

We can predict how unstable nuclei might decay with some accuracy just by comparing their position on an N v Z diagram (Segre chart).

On an N-Z diagram nuclei to the lower right of the valley of stability will tend to beta minus decay whereas nuclei to the upper left will tend to beta plus (positron) decay and nuclei above Z = 82 may alpha decay and still heavier ones may undergo spontaneous fission (see diagram). Other, more exotic, decay modes are known but are beyond the scope of this treatment.

Further reading: reference 122 gives a succinct description of 11 types of radioactive decay.

A.10. Mass defect

This section explains why the fission process produces energy in terms of the mass defect of bound nuclei. It is not entirely necessary to understand this section to understand the Chernobyl accident so long as you accept the statement that "some heavy nuclei can be induced to fission if hit by a neutron and in doing so give off fission fragments, neutrons and energy".

In the "real" world of every day experience mass and energy are conserved. The "conservation laws" (conservation of energy, of momentum and of angular momentum) are very useful for helping us predict outcomes of experiments where energy is transformed from, for example, kinetic energy to potential energy. They do not apply in the same way in the world of the very small and the very fast. Here energy and mass are interchangeable as shown in one of the most famous equations:

$$E = mc^2$$

The masses of atoms are conveniently expressed in terms of the atomic mass unit (u), which is defined as being exactly one-twelfth the mass of a ^{12}C atom. Given that 12g of ^{12}C is a mol and contains N_A atoms. The weight of one ^{12}C atom is 12/6.022 140 76 × 10^{23} kg = 1.9923 x 10^{-26} kg and one amu is therefore 1/12 of this or 1.6605 x 10^{-27} kg.

The *mole* (mol) is the SI unit for the amount of substance.

The *mole* was defined as the amount of substance containing the same number of chemical units (atoms, molecules, ions, electrons or groups of entities) as exactly 12 grams of carbon-12. From 20th May 2019 the Avogadro constant N_A is defined as 6.022 140 76 × 10^{23} mol^{-1} (Ref. 123). So one mole now contains exactly 6.022 140 76 × 10^{23} elementary entities.

The mass of atomic nuclei can be measured to high precision using, for example, a mass spectrometer. In these devices the sample to be analysed is vapourised into a vacuum, ionised in an electric field (some of the outer electrons removed to give a positive ion), accelerated through an electric field so that the ions of same charge have a narrow range of velocities and then passed into and through a magnetic field. The charged particle is deflected by the magnetic field to a degree determined by its "magnetic rigidity". This magnetic rigidity can be inferred by detecting by how much the particle was deflected. Different experimental set-ups can have the magnetic field varied and a fixed detector, or the magnetic field constant and either a moving detector or a position sensitive detector which gives a measurement related to position along a line (1 dimension) or a plane (2 dimensions). See Table 9.

Particle	Mass (kg)	Mass (u)	Mass (Mev/c²)
1 atomic mass unit	1.660540 x 10^{-27} kg	1.000 u	931.5 MeV/c²
neutron	1.674929 x 10^{-27} kg	1.008664 u	939.57 MeV/c²
proton	1.672623 x 10^{-27} kg	1.007276 u	938.28 MeV/c²
electron	9.109390 x 10^{-31} kg	0.00054858 u	0.511 MeV/c²

Table 9 Accurate masses of sub-atomic particles (Ref. 124)

It is noticeable that the atomic mass unit is defined as 1/12th the mass of carbon-12 which is composed of 6 neutrons and 6 protons, each of which has a mass of slightly greater than 1 unit. When carbon-2 is formed from 12 separate nucleons mass is lost.

When nuclear masses are measured accurately they are always found to be less than the summed mass of the neutrons and protons that they are made of. To break the nucleus into its constituent protons, neutrons and electrons you would have to provide this amount of energy. This *mass defect* is a measure of the *binding energy* of the nucleus.

For a neutral atom the equation for mass defect is:

$$\text{Mass defect} = [\, Z(m_p + m_e) + (A-Z)m_n \,] - M$$

Where:

m_p	Mass of proton (u)
m_n	Mass of neutron (u)
m_e	Mass of electron (u)
M	Mass of neutral atom (u)

(This is saying that the mass defect is equal to the summed mass of the constituent bits minus the mass of the ensemble)

Nucleon masses have been measured to very high precision.

Proton mass $1.007276466879 \pm 0.000000000091$ u (Ref. 126);
Neutron mass $1.00866491588 \pm 0.00000000049$ u (Ref. 127).

The mass defect can be converted into energy using $E = mc^2$

Where	E	is the energy in Joules (J)
	m	is the mass in kilograms (kg)
	c	is the velocity of light in $m.s^{-1}$ (2.998×10^8 $m.s^{-1}$)

Since $u = 1.661 \times 10^{-27}$ this gives $E(J) = m(u) \times 1.493 \times 10^{-10}$ J

In the context of nuclear physics we more usually express energy in units of MeV (mega electron volts) where 1 MeV $= 1.602 \times 10^{-13}$ J so:

$E(MeV) = m(u) \times 931.9$ i.e. an energy of 931.9 MeV is created when 1 amu is converted to energy.

A.11. Binding Energy per Nucleon

A useful quantity is the mean binding energy per nucleon for which a simple shortcut is:

$$BE/A = (931/A) \times [1.00794\, Z + 1.008664\, (A-Z) - M]$$

Where the mass of the hydrogen atom (1.00794 u $\pm$ 0.00001 u) and mass of the neutron in atomic mass units (1.008664 u) are used.

A plot of binding energy per nucleon is shown as Figure 30. This is based on a large dataset of binding energy against mass number. Each dot is a data point. The red lines joins the data for the most stable of each mass number and is there merely to guide the eye. The general shape of this dataset tells us a number of things. Binding energy per nucleon peaks at between mass number of 50 and 100. For nuclei heavier than this it is energetically favourable to fission. For nuclei lighter than this it is energetically favourable to fuse (small nuclei joining together to produce a larger one). In this dataset 62-Ni has the highest binding energy per nucleon at 8794.553 keV.

The binding energy per nucleon is a measure of stability of the nucleus. The larger the binding energy per nucleon, the greater the work that must be done to remove the nucleons from the nucleus and therefore the more stable the nucleus is.

Example: Given that the binding energies per nucleon for ^{235}U, ^{140}Xe and ^{92}Sr are 7.59 MeV, 8.29 MeV and 8.65 MeV respectively, calculate the energy released when ^{235}U undergoes spontaneous fission to ^{140}Xe, ^{92}Sr and 3 neutrons.

$$_{92}^{235}\text{U} \longrightarrow {}_{54}^{140}\text{Xe} + {}_{38}^{92}\text{Sr} + 3\,{}_{0}^{1}\text{n}$$

Energy released = binding energy of ^{140}Xe + binding energy of ^{54}Sr - binding energy of ^{235}U = 140 x 8.29+ 92 x 8.65 - 235 x 7.59 = 173 MeV (Nuclear data from Ref. 131)

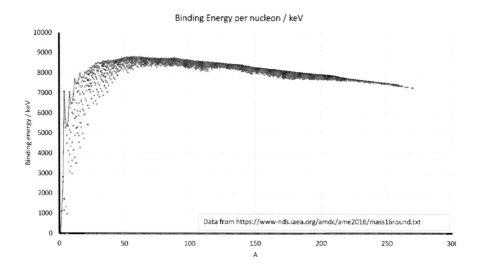

Figure 30 Binding energy per nucleon

A.12. Availability of nuclear data

There are many compilations of nuclear data available on the internet. A very comprehensive collection can be found on the national Nuclear Data Centre (Brookhaven National Laboratory) web-site (Ref. 128).

The chart of the nuclides option gives you a classic Segre chart view from which you can select isotopes and see their atomic mass excess Δ (MeV) defined as:

$$\Delta(z,n) = (Mass(z,n) - A) \times amu$$

where

Mass(z,n) is the mass in atomic mass units of a nuclei (z,n);

amu $\quad = Mass(6,6)/12$ $\qquad\qquad$ $Mass(6,6) = Mass\ ^{12}C$

Kaye and Laby on-line is a comprehensive data set provided by the UK National Physical Laboratory (Ref. 129).

A simple machine readable table can be found on the IAEA website (Ref. 130).

Appendix B Additional reactor physics

B.1 Delayed neutrons and small changes in reactivity

In Section 4.3.4 the role of delayed neutrons in reactor control was introduced. This section looks at the matter in a bit more detail.

We will now look at the build-up of the neutron population when there is an injection of reactivity to a critical reactor and delayed neutrons are taken into account.

Returning to our reactor with a fraction β of the neutrons being delayed and a neutron density of N_0. When the reactor is critical we have $(1 - \beta)N_0$ prompt neutrons and βN_0 delayed neutron being produced and lost in each cycle.

Now consider a step increase in reactivity Δk. This causes an immediate change in the number of prompt neutrons being produced but, while it increases the rate of delayed neutron precursors being produced it does not result in an immediate change in delayed neutron production.

In the next generation there will be $N_1 = N_0(1+\Delta k)$ neutrons, of which $(1 - \beta)N_0(1 + \Delta k)$ prompt neutrons which will be joined by βN_0 delayed neutrons from existing precursors. There will also be $(1+\Delta k)\beta$ new delayed neutron precursors produced.

The number of neutrons in the second generation is therefore:

$N_1 = (1 - \beta)N_0(1 + \Delta k) + \beta N_0$.

It can be seen that the number of neutrons in successive generations, assuming that the number of delayed neutrons entering the system remains unchanged is:

$$N_{x+1} = (1-\beta)N_x(1+\Delta k) + \beta N_0$$

This equation can be used repeatedly to show how the prompt neutron density changes with generations.

This works well in a spreadsheet. Consider a critical reactor with a neutron population of 1,000,000 and delayed neutron fraction of 0.007. This is composed of $(1 - \beta)N = 993,000$ prompt neutrons and $\beta N = 7,000$ delayed neutrons in each generation.

Now inject $\Delta k = 0.005$.

In the next generation there will be 1,005,000 neutrons ($N_1 = N_0 k$) of which 997965 will be prompt neutrons ($N_1 (1-\beta)$), which would be joined by 7,000 delayed neutrons from previously generated precursors, and 7035 new neutron precursors ($N_1 \beta$) will be generated.

We can progress this treatment on through the generations assuming that the increased numbers of precursors does not lead to an increase in delayed neutrons for many generations of prompt neutrons. A spreadsheet shows this in action (Figure 31).

We see that the number of prompt neutrons increases rapidly at first but then levels off. This is referred to as "the prompt jump".

It can be shown that the amplitude of the prompt jump is given by:

$$\frac{N}{N_0} = \frac{\beta}{\beta - \Delta k}$$

Reactor designers and operators attempt to limit the amount of reactivity that can be added at one time. This is done by, for example, limiting the speed at which rods can be withdrawn and the number of rods that can be withdrawn at the same time. The operators of PWRs have to be careful not to add a large volume of cold water or a large volume of water with lower boron concentration than is currently in the circuit to the cooling circuits too quickly for the same reason.

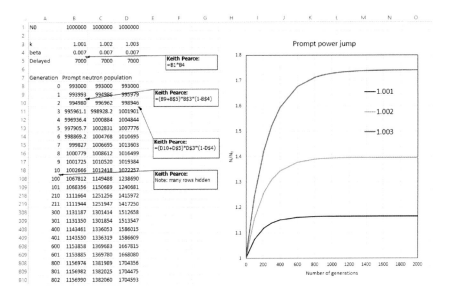

Figure 31 Prompt jump

This next section shows that the power of a reactor will grow exponentially if k_{eff} is greater than 1. This is a result you can accept on trust if you are uncomfortable with the mathematics.

After the prompt jump the neutron population continues to grow exponentially as the delayed neutrons begin to increase.

The change in neutron density from one generation to the next can be written:

$$\Delta N = kN - N$$

With N neutrons in one generation and kN in the next.

By definition this takes place in one neutron lifetime l giving:

$$\frac{\Delta N}{\Delta t} = \frac{kN-N}{l}$$

Or

$$\frac{dN}{dt} = \frac{kN-N}{l} = \frac{N}{l}(k-1) = \frac{N}{l}\delta k$$

Which has solution:

$$N(t) = N_0 e^{\left(\frac{\delta k}{l}\right)t}$$

N(t)   Number density of neutrons at time t (neutrons/cm^3)
N$_0$ Number density of neutrons at time t=0 (neutrons/cm^3)

δk	(1-k)
k	Relative change in neutron number density per cycle (dimensionless)
l	Cycle time (average neutron lifetime, fission to fission) s

This equation shows that the population of neutrons will change exponentially if the number of fissions induced by the neutrons from a single fission reaction are on average not equal to one. The two important parameters in this exponential are the ratio of neutrons between successive generations and the time between generations which control the rate of increase.

It can be shown that the period of the long term neutron flux increase following the prompt jump is given by:

$$\tau = \frac{\beta - \delta k}{\lambda \, \delta k}$$

where $\lambda = {}^{1}/_{l}$ is the average decay constant of delayed neutron precursors, which is about 0.08 s^{-1} for the table of precursors given above.

τ is the period of the reactor (the time it takes power to increase by a factor of e (2.718) (Ref. 132)

After the prompt jump the neutron population rises exponentially depending on the neutron lifecycle time and the reactivity.

$$\phi(t) = \phi(0)e^{t/\tau}$$

The change of neutron population with time following a small injection of reactivity is shown in Figure 12.

Delayed neutrons make reactor control possible by giving the operators and the automatic control systems much more time to respond to changes in reactivity but they complicate reactor analysis because it is necessary to model the change in the concentrations of the neutron emitters with time following a reactivity change and the effects of neutrons with a range of energies being emitted during a range of times following the initial fission. In real reactors these parameters can all vary with burn-up.

B.2   Fission reaction in more detail

The picture we have of this fission process is that the U-235 nucleus is initially reasonably spherical but additional energy from the absorption of a neutron and the combination of the short range attractive forces and long range repulsive forces result in an increasing deformation where the nucleus becomes elongated, which further weakness the effect of the short range forces. The nucleus then forms into a barbell shape and then into two overlapping spheres which separate pushed apart by the Coulomb repulsion between the protons. A simple liquid drop model, where the nucleus is treated as a drop of water, would predict that the two fission fragments would be about the same size. However, deeper nuclear structure phenomena mean that an asymetic split is more likely as this leads to more tightly bound fission fragments.

Looking at the masses on each side of these equations

U-235 + n > Ba-144 + Kr-90 + 2n

235.043928 + 1.008664 > 143.922955 + 89.919527 + (2 x 1.008664)

236.052592 > 235.85981

Mass difference 0.192728 AMU or 179.65 MeV

U-235 + n > Zr-94 + Te-139 + 3n

236.052592 > 93.906312 + 138.935367 + (3 x 1.008664)

> 235.867671

Mass difference = 0.184921 AMU = 172.32 MeV

Kaye and Laby (Ref. 129) Section 4.7.1 give the average values shown in Table 10.

Instantaneously released energy	U-233	U-235	Pu-239
Kinetic energy of fission fragments	168.2 MeV	169.1 MeV	175.8 MeV
Kinetic energy of prompt neutrons	4.9	4.8	5.9
Energy of prompt gamma rays	7.7	7.0	7.8
Energy from decaying fission fragments			
Energy of beta particles	5.2	6.5	5.3
Energy of anti-neutrinos	6.9	8.8	7.1
Energy of delayed gammas	5.0	6.3	5.2
Total	197.9	202.5	207.1

Table 10 Fission energy distribution

In an operating reactor, all of the energy other than that of the anti-neutrinos, is eventually converted to heat in the reactor core or its surrounding shield material. Some additional energy is obtained from the binding energy of captured (non-fission) neutrons. For thermal reactors this is about 9.1, 8.8 and 11.5 MeV for U-233, U-235 and Pu-239 respectively.

The fission fragments are almost always unstable and decay sometime later giving off both radiation and heat. Both of these attributes cause problems for reactor designers and operators. The radioactive fission fragments must be isolated from the environment pretty much indefinitely and the heat, called "decay heat" in this context, can be sufficient to damage the fuel unless adequate cooling is provided for an extended period after the reactor has shut-down.

Figure 32 shows the fission product yield (in percentage) against mass number. The data was taken from the IAEA Nuclear Data Services (https://www-nds.iaea.org/). This is often shown as a tidier "double hump". The maxima are at about mass number of 90 and 140. The lower hump provides molybdenum, strontium and krypton and the second hump provides iodine, caesium and xenon, among others, as high yield fission products.

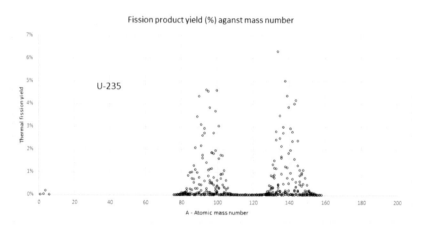

Figure 32 Fission product yield v mass number

What is the probability that a neutron moving through a medium will induce a fission? Consider an array of U-235 atoms in a uranium dioxide fuel pellet being bombarded by a beam of neutrons. We may assume that the rate at which reactions between U-235 and neutrons is proportional to the number of each of them there i.e. the more U-235 atoms in the space and the more neutrons passing into it then the more interactions there will be.

Let us assume that the density of U-235 atoms is N atoms per cubic centimetre, and the flux of neutrons is Φ neutrons per centimetre squared per second. We can guess that the reaction rate RR (reactions per second) is proportional to the product of these two values:

$$RR \propto \Phi.N$$

Where

     RR   Reaction rate, $cm^{-3} s^{-1}$, (reactions per cm^3 per s)

     Φ Neutron flux, neutrons $cm^{-2} s^{-1}$, (neutrons per cm^2 per s)

     N   Target density, cm^{-3} (atoms per cm^{-3})

This can be rearranged to give

$$RR = \sigma.\Phi.N$$

Where we have introduced a constant of proportionality σ which we can easily show has dimensions of area (cm^2) and which we call the "cross section".

"Cross section" is the term used to describe the probability of a nuclear interaction.

The **microscopic cross section** represents the effective target area of a single target nucleus for an incident particle. The units are given in cm^2 or barns (1b = $10^{-28} m^2$ or $10^{-24} cm^2$).

The **macroscopic cross section** (Σ) represents the effective target area of all nuclei within the volume of interest ($\Sigma = \sigma.N$) with units of cm^{-1} (so it is not really correct to call it a cross-section).

Knowing the rate of reaction (RR) and the energy produced per reaction (about 200 MeV per fission) we can now relate the power density of the reactor to the neutron density.

$$PD = 200.\sigma.\Phi.N$$

Where

     PD = Power Density   MeV $cm^{-3} s^{-1}$

Now, since 1 $MeV.s^{-1}$ = 1.602 x 10^{-13} W

     PD = 3.2 x $10^{-11}.\sigma.\Phi.N$ [W.cm^{-3}]

Giving the power density in W cm^{-3} for a target density of N cm^{-3}, a neutron flux of Φ neutrons $cm^{-2} s^{-1}$ and a cross section of reaction of σ cm^2.

This shows that, at any time, the power density of a reactor is proportional to the neutron flux (as you might expect). The constant of proportionality may change with time and with position in the reactor as the target density changes as the fuel is burned up and the number of fissile targets changes.

While simplistically you might expect that when you load fuel into the reactor there is a certain number of fissile target atoms and these are used up in a well behaved linear manner that is not necessarily true. Some heavy isotopes are not fissile but are able to capture a neutron and produce a fissile daughter or grand-daughter product. These are called *fertile isotopes* and they include 238-U and and 233-Th.

For example: Absorption of a neutron in the 238-U nucleus yields 239-U. This decays (beta decay) to 239-Np (neptunium) (half-life 2.36 days). 239-Np decays (beta decay) to 239-Pu (plutonium) (half-life 2.36 days) which is fissile.

n + 238-U $\longrightarrow$ 239-U $\longrightarrow$ 239-Np + β $\longrightarrow$ 239-Pu + β

B.3   Neutron capture cross section

Having introduced the concept of the "cross section" being a measure of the probability of a nuclear reaction taking place we will now look at some real data about the magnitude of these cross sections.

The data for Figure 33 were taken from the NEA nuclear data services system (Ref. 136) using the "search the evaluated database", selecting Incident neutron data, TLS JEF-3.1.2, 92(U), 235, reaction cross section and (n,f) and then downloading the data and plotting it in excel (it is possible to down load and present a great deal of data!).

At low energies the cross section is proportional to 1/v, where v is the velocity of the neutron. This can be understood as, in this range, the slower neutron is travelling the more time it has to interact with the nucleus and therefore more likelihood of interaction.

It is important to notice that the vertical axis on this diagram is logarithmic - neutron capture cross sections depend strongly on the energy of the neutron and are far more likely at low energies.

The rapid changes in cross section between about 10^{-6} MeV and 10^{-3} MeV are called "resonances". When the energy that the neutron will contribute to the nucleus (binding energy + kinetic energy) equals an energy level in the resultant nucleus the probability of absorption increases significantly because the system does not have to manage the mismatch in energy.

It should be noted that for U-235 the probability of the (n,f) reaction is significantly higher at low energies than at high. However, fission tends to produce high energy neutrons with most of them having energies about 1 MeV (See spectrum below). This is why many reactor designs use a "moderator" to slow down the neutrons produced by fission. These are collectively called "thermal reactors" as opposed to "fast reactors".

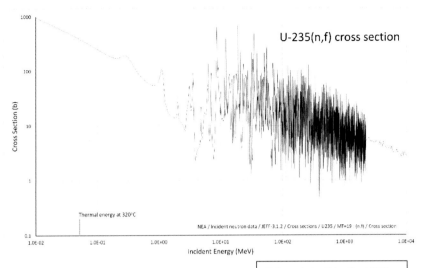

Figure 33 Fission cross section U-235

Note: x-axis should be eV not MeV

Because of the high resonance absorption cross section in U-238 it is advantageous to moderate the neutrons away from the fuel. This is one reason why reactor designs tend to have fuel and moderator separated; a homogeneous reactor[46] would almost certainly lose more neutrons to resonance capture than one with a well-chosen *pitch* between the fuel elements.

B.4   Mean free path

So how likely is a neutron to interact with material that it passes through? We can try to answer this using the concept of the *mean free path* (usually denoted by λ).

The *Mean free path* is defined as the average distance between collisions (or interactions). For neutrons - the average distance a neutron will travel before undergoing a particular interaction.

If a neutron has a probability of undergoing a particular interaction in one centimetre of travel (which is what the macroscopic cross section tells us), then the reciprocal of this value describes how far the neutron will travel on average before undergoing an interaction of that type. That is:

$$\lambda = \frac{1}{\Sigma}$$

Where   λ   mean free path (cm)

---

[46] A homogeneous reactor is one in which the fuel, moderator and coolant are all be mixed uniformly (Ref. 135).

$$\Sigma \qquad \text{Macroscopic cross section (cm}^{-1})$$

For a material composed of several species

$$\Sigma = N_1\sigma_1 + N_2\sigma_2 + N_3\sigma_3 + N_4\sigma_4 + \ldots\ldots$$

Where $\qquad N_n \qquad$ Number density of the nth species

$\qquad\qquad\qquad \sigma_n \qquad$ Microscopic cross section for reaction with n^{th} species

This quantity is also known as the relaxation length, because it is the distance in which the intensity of the neutrons that have not caused a reaction has decreased with a factor e.

Example: Estimate the mean free path of neutrons in a boron carbide control rod.

Data: $\qquad\qquad$ Boron carbide (B_4C) has a density of 2.52 g/cm^3
$\qquad\qquad\qquad$ Natural boron is 80.1% 11-B and 19.9% 10-B
$\qquad\qquad\qquad \sigma_T(^{10}B) = 3848$ b
$\qquad\qquad\qquad \sigma_T(^{11}B) = 5.067$ b
$\qquad\qquad\qquad \sigma_T(^{12}C) = 4.952$ b

[Cross section data from the TENDL-2017 database via Nuclear Energy Agency (Ref. 136)]

We can first estimate the number density of each type of nucleus.

Number of molecules of B_4C in one centimetre cubed is given by Avogadro's number and the atomic masses. [Atomic mass of boron = (0.801 x 10) + (0.199 x 11) = 10.8]

$$N_{B4C} = \text{(2.52 g/cm}^3) \times (6.02\times10^{23} \text{ nuclei/mol)/ (4} \times 10.8 + 1\times12$$
g/mol)

$$= 2.75\times10^{22} \text{ molecules of B4C/cm}^3$$

Number of carbon-12 atoms: 2.75×10^{22} /cm^3

Number of boron-11 atoms: $0.801 \times 4 \times 2.75\times10^{22} = 8.80\times10^{22}$ atoms of ^{11}B/cm^3

Number of boron-10 atoms: $0.199 \times 4 \times 2.75\times10^{22} = 2.18\times10^{22}$ atoms of ^{10}B/cm^3

The macroscopic cross-section is then:

$$\Sigma t_{B4C} = 3848\times10^{-24} \times 2.18\times10^{22} + 5.677\times10^{-24} \times 8.80\times10^{22} + 4.952\times10^{-24} \times 2.75\times10^{22}$$
$$= 84.5 \text{ cm}^{-1}$$

And the mean free path is:

$$\lambda_t = 1/\Sigma t_{B4C} = 0.012 \text{ cm} = 0.12 \text{ mm}$$

Remembering that the number of neutrons is reduced by a factor of 1/e (0.3679) for each mean free path, we see that a boron carbide rod will absorb most of the neutrons that hit it. [Transmission through 1 cm thickness = 0.3679 ** (10.0/0.12) = 6.5×10^{-37}].

Boron Carbide is a good material for a control rod because it is very good at absorbing neutrons and survives reactor conditions reasonably well without too much change in shape or wearing. Rods are replaced when a given fraction of their boron has been burned out or when they show too much wear.

B.5 Moderator

Moderators are used in nuclear reactors to slow fast neutrons down so that they are more likely to initiate a fission in U-235.

The way to take kinetic energy out of a neutron is to make it collide with another nucleus and bounce off making the other nucleus recoil, taking a share of the kinetic energy, and possibly leaving the target nucleus in an excited state, taking the energy of excitation. These scattering modes are called "elastic scattering" (momentum and kinetic energy are conserved - consider snooker balls colliding) or "inelastic scattering" (where momentum is conserved as is the sum of kinetic energy and the excitation energy). A thermal neutron is one that has a velocity that is acquired by elastic collisions with the material around it and therefore has a similar velocity to the atoms in the material.

The most effective way to lose energy in a single collision is to collide with a particle of the same mass. (Consider how much you can slow a snooker ball down by hitting it into a stationary snooker ball and then try the same trick with a target ball that is considerably heavier - the incident ball bounces back with its kinetic energy pretty much intact - the target ball hardly moves). So we want our moderator have similar mass to the neutron.

We also want our neutron to survive the collision. The ideal moderator would have a low cross-section for neutron absorption.

We need the moderator to have suitable physical and chemical properties so that they can be built into our reactor. It would also be nice if they were cheap, plentiful and not toxic.

Table 11 summarises the properties for a range of candidate materials (treatment and data based on Ref. 42).

	Mass	Abundance	Form	Capture X-sec (b)	
Hydrogen	1	99.9885%	Light water	0.644	Good
	2	0.0115%	Heavy water	0.0013	candidate
Helium	3	Low	Gas		Density
	4	> 99.99%			too low
Lithium	6	7.6%	Solid	70.56	Neutron
	7	92.4%			absorber
Beryllium	8	100%	Solid	0.0076	Okay but toxic
Boron	10	20%	Solid	764.9	Neutron
	11	80%			absorber
Carbon	12	99%	Solid	0.00337	Good
	13	1%			candidate

Table 11 properties of moderator candidates

Hydrogen is ideal from the point of view of having near identical mass to the neutron so involves the best energy transfer per collision. This can conveniently be used in the form of water. Heavy water, which has hydrogen-2 (deuterium) in it has a much lower neutron absorption cross-section which more than repays for its mass mismatch. It is, however, harder to obtain.

Lithium and boron suffer from having a neutron absorption cross section that is too high.

Carbon is another good candidate. It is not such a good mass match as hydrogen so more collisions are needed to achieve thermalisation but a much lower neutron absorption cross section then normal water which compensates for this. Carbon can be produced in bulk with acceptable purity in the form of graphite[47]. An issue with solid moderators, that is absent with liquid moderators, is that they are subject to corrosion and ablation, both of which must be managed.

B.6 Decay heat

The importance of decay heat for nuclear reactor safety was illustrated all too clearly at Fukushima on Friday 11th of March 2011 when almost all site power was lost in the aftermath of the Great East Japan Earthquake and the large tsunami it created. The three reactors on site all shutdown with no significant damage when the earthquake struck. But nearly an hour after the earthquake the tsunami arrived and disabled

---

[47] Graphite is not without its problems as a moderator. (1) It changes shape and size when subject to varying temperatures and radiation fields. (2) A process called Wigner Energy, in which neutron induced dislocations in the graphite structure leads to the storage of energy, was a cause of the Windscale fire (Ref. 134).

almost all of the site's power supplies and some important heat exchangers. At this stage the reactors' decay heat production would have been about 1.5% of full power. With heat being added faster than the compromised cooling systems could remove it the cores began to heat up. Sixteen hours after the shutdown the reactor 1 core melted. Reactor two lasted maybe 100 hours. Reactor three is thought to have melted on the Sunday. Decay heat had written off three reactors and caused extensive environmental harm.

There are several sources of decay heat in a nuclear reactor:

- Decay of unstable fission products;
- Decay of unstable actinides formed by neutron capture in uranium and plutonium isotopes within the fuel;
- Fissions produced by delayed neutrons;
- Activation products in the reactor structures;
- Spontaneous fissions and radioactive decays in the nuclear fuel.

Of these the decay of unstable fission products is the main source of heat for a period lasting up to years with actinide decay dominating in the long term.

As the reactor is operating fission products, activation products and actinides are produced by neutron interactions. These products decay with their characteristic half-life and some may be removed by further neutron interactions. If the reactor is operating for long enough then the short lived species will reach an equilibrium in which their creation rate is matched by their destruction rate as was found for Xe-135 in Section 4.3.5. The long lived nuclei will continue to increase for longer, many will never reach equilibrium. An exact solution to the decay heat curve would have to take into account that there are hundreds of radioactive species in an operating reactor, each with their own concentration, half-life and decay mode. Decay heat is therefore modelled as a sum of exponential functions with different half-lives and different initial heat contributions.

When the reactor is scrammed these fission products, activation products and actinides continue to decay with a very wide range of half-lives. Beta particles produced by radioactive decay deposit their energy close to their point of creation, so most of the beta energy will be found in the fuel. Gamma radiation has a longer range and will deposit energy in the fuel, moderator and reactor structures, particularly in the high density, high Z (large atoms with more protons) material such as fuel.

Decay heat is a long term issue for the nuclear industry affecting reactor design, used fuel handling, used fuel storage and reprocessing.

A detailed but clear description of the mathematics of decay heat can be found in Ref. 137.

B.7   Further reading

For reactor physics I refer to Nuclear Reactor Engineering, 3rd Edition by Glasstone and Sesonske (Ref. 138) although this is now rather old. I've also enjoyed reading Nuclear Reactor Physics by E.E.Lewis, which is a more modern text (Ref. 139).

Appendix C - Jargon buster

Technical terms

Term	Explanation
atom	The basic building block of chemical elements. They consist of protons and neutrons bound together in a nucleus with electrons "orbiting" at a relatively large distance (See Section 4.1).
Base load	A term used in electricity generation and distribution used to denote the minimum demand over a period, usually a day. This can be met by unresponsive generators.
chain reaction	In reactor physics used to describe the manner in which neutrons produced in a fission reaction can go on to induce more fissions in a repeating cycle.
control rods	Devices to control the fission chain reaction in a nuclear reactor by absorbing more neutrons if inserted further into the reactor or fewer neutrons if withdrawn.
coolant	The fluid that takes the heat from the nuclear fuel and delivers it outside the core.
decay heat	Energy produced by the radioactive decay of fission fragments. See section 5.7.
delayed neutrons	Neutrons produced by the decay of fission fragments that are released sometime after the fission event. These are important for the control of reactors. See section 4.3.4.
enriching or enrichment	Enrichment is the process of increasing the proportion of U-235 in a fuel. Natural uranium contains only 0.7% of the U-235 isotope. The remaining 99.3% is mostly U-238 which does not contribute directly to the fission process. Enrichments in the range 0.7% - 5% are common in commercial reactors.
fission	In nuclear physics, the splitting of a large nucleus into fission fragments (smaller nuclei), free neutrons, radiation and energy.

fission fragments	The remnants of the fission of a large nucleus. Usually two, but sometimes three, nuclei that are almost always unstable.
isotope	An atomic form of an element having a particular number of neutrons. Different isotopes of an element have the same number of protons but different numbers of neutrons and hence different atomic masses, e.g. U-235 and U-238, each with 92 protons and with 143 and 146 neutrons respectively.
macroscopic cross section (Σ)	The effective target area of all nuclei within the volume of interest ($\Sigma = \sigma . N$) with units of cm^{-1} (so it is not really correct to call it a cross-section).
microscopic cross section	The effective target area of a single target nucleus for an incident particle. The units are given in cm^2 or barns (1b = 10^{-28} m^2 or 10^{-24} cm^2).
Mean free path	The average distance between collisions (or interactions).
moderate	In nuclear reactors the action of slowing down fission neutrons to make them more likely to induce further fissions. See section B.5.
moderater	A material such as light or heavy water or graphite used in a reactor to slow down fast neutrons by collision with lighter nuclei so as to expedite further fission. See section B.5.
Mole (mol)	The *mole* (mol) SI unit for the amount of substance. One mole contains exactly 6.022 140 76 × 10^{23} elementary entities.
neutron	A sub-atomic particle with a mass slightly greater than that of a proton and no electric charge. See section 4.1.
neutron economy	A term used in the discussion of the possible fates of fission neutrons (leakage, absorption and fission). See section 4.3.
neutron poisons	Isotopes that have a high cross-section for neutron absorption and therefore remove neutrons from reactors. Used in control rods and appear as fission fragments. See section 4.3.5.
nuclear reactor	A device used to initiate and control a self-sustained nuclear chain reaction.

non-fission absorption	Absorption of a neutron that does not result in a fission.
pitch	The distance between the central axes of 2 neighbouring fuel elements. Usually are chosen to give optimum balance between moderation and absorption.
Prompt Neutron Lifetime	The average time from a prompt neutron emission to either its absorption (fission or radiative capture) or to its escape from the system.
proton	A sub-atomic particle with a mass slightly less than that of a neutron and having an electric charge of +e. See section 4.1.
Radioactive decay	The process where an unstable nuclei spontaneously rearranges itself, losing energy and emitting radiation.
Resonance	Some nuclear reactions, such as neutron induced fission, are much more likely to happen if the incident particle has an energy close to anyone of a number of certain narrowly defined values. These energy values are referred to as resonance energies (see Section B.3)
Scram	A system to release all of the control rods above a reactor into the core to quickly shut the chain reaction down.
Sub-cooling	The difference in temperature between the cooling water at the reactor inlets and the boiling point of water at that pressure.
Strong force	The force between nucleons (neutrons and protons). It is repulsive at very short distances (up to 1 fm) but strongly attractive over distances comparable with the size of a nucleus (a few fm). [1 fm = 10^{-15} m]
the infinite multiplication factor	The ratio of number of neutrons in one generation of the chain reaction to the number of neutrons in the previous generation for a theoretical system with no leakage. Can be expressed in the four factor formula: $k_\infty = \eta.f.\rho.\epsilon$ section 4.3.1.
thermal neutrons	Thermal neutrons are so called because they have a similar kinetic energy to the atoms or molecules around them and so

	are at the same temperature. Thermal neutrons have a range of energies clustered around 0.04 eV.
	A thermal neutron is one that has a velocity that is acquired by elastic collisions with the material around it.
	See section B.5.
Void coefficient of reactivity	A rate of change in the reactivity of a water reactor system resulting from a formation of steam bubbles as the power level and temperature increase.
	US NCR Lexicon (Ref. 72)
Xenon transient	A phenomenon seen in nuclear reactors when the power density changes. Xe-135 is produced in reactors as a fission fragment and as a decay product of a fission fragment. It has a high neutron absorption cross-section and therefore is a neutron poison. At stable power levels the amount of Xe-135 reaches an equilibrium value where its creation rate balances its destruction rate. A reduction in power results in a temporary increase in Xe-135 levels which reduces the reactivity of the system making criticality harder to achieve while the transient lasts. See section 4.3.5.

Mathematical symbols used

Σ_F	Macroscopic thermal fission cross section of the fuel (cm^2)
c	The velocity of light in $m.s^{-1}$ (2.998×10^8 $m.s^{-1}$)
E	Energy, Normally measured in joules (J) but in atomic and nuclear physics the electron volt (eV) or multipliers keV (1000 eV) and MeV (1,000,000 eV) are used for convenience.
f	Thermal utilisation factor. The fraction of thermal neutrons that induce fission in a reactor core.
h	The Planck constant, $6.626\ 070\ 15 \times 10^{-34}$ J.s
K	The Boltzmann constant, $k = 8.52 \cdot 10\text{-}5$ eV/K. relates the average relative kinetic energy of particles in a gas with the temperature of the gas. E = kT where T is the temperature in kelvin.

k or k_{eff}	The effective multiplication factor (ratio of number of neutrons in each cycle of the chain reaction) be expressed as: $$k = \frac{\text{Rate of neutron production}}{\text{Rate of neutron absorption} + \text{rate of leakage}}$$
m	The mass of the particle (kg)
M	Mass of neutral atom (u)
m_e	Mass of electron (u)
m_n	Mass of neutron (u)
m_p	Mass of proton (u)
n	Neutron
N	Target density, cm^{-3}, (atoms per cm^{-3})
N_I	Number density of I-135 nuclei (cm^{-3})
N_{Xe}	Number density of Xe-135 nuclei (cm^{-3})
P	Reactor power
P_{FNL}	Fast non-leakage fraction. The probability that a fast neutron will NOT leak from a reactor.
P_{TNL}	Thermal non-leakage probability. The probability that a thermal neutron will NOT leak from a reactor.
RR	Reaction rate, $cm^{-3} s^{-1}$, (reactions per cm^3 per s)
T	Temperature on kelvin scale in which absolute temperature is 0 degrees (-217.16°C)
v	The velocity of a particle $(m.s^{-2})$
Y_I	Cumulative Fission fragment yield of I-135 (0.061)
Y_{Xe}	Fission fragment yield of Xe-135 (0.003)
β	The delayed neutron fraction. The fraction of fission neutrons that result from the radioactive decay of fission products. Generally about 0.065% for U-235. Importantly, if the reactivity of a reactor approaches this value it goes "prompt critical" and power rises uncontrollably.

δk	(1-k)
ε	The fast fission factor, The total number of fast neutrons being produced divided by the number of fast neutrons being produced by thermal fission.
η	Reproduction factor. The number of neutron produced by fuel divided by the number absorbed by fuel.
λ	The wavelength of a wave or particle (m)
λ_I	Decay constant for I-135 (s^{-1}) 2.9 x 10^{-5} s^{-1}
λ_{Xe}	Decay constant for Xe-135 (s^{-1}) 2.1 x 10^{-5} s^{-1}
p	The resonance escape probability. The probability of a neutron avoiding resonance capture during its slowing down phase in the neutron chain reaction cycle.
ρ	Reactivity (of a nuclear reactor) $\rho = \frac{k_{eff}-1}{k_{eff}}$
σ^I_a	Cross section for absorbtion of thermal neutron by I-135 - 4.8 b
σ^{Xe}_a	Cross section for absorbtion of thermal neutron by Xe-135 - 3.0 x 10^6 b
Φ	Neutron flux, neutrons cm^{-2} s^{-1}, (neutrons per cm^2 per s)

References

1. Various sources including Bulletin of Atomic Scientists, September 1986, https://books.google.co.uk/books?id=ngYAAAAAMBAJ&printsec=frontcover&source=gbs_ge_summary_r&cad=0#v=onepage&q&f=false and New York Times http://movies2.nytimes.com/learning/general/onthisday/big/0426.html#article

2. YouTube, Compilation of Rare 1986 Videos of Chernobyl Disaster. (English), https://www.youtube.com/watch?v=Cc-vvhWXL9Q

3. Semenov, B.A., "Nuclear Power in the Soviet Union", IAEA Bulletin, Vol. 25, No.2, June 1983. https://www.iaea.org/sites/default/files/25204744759.pdf

4. Zheludev and Konstabtinov, Nuclear Power in the USSR, IAEA Bulletin, Vol. 22, No.2, 1980, https://www.iaea.org/sites/default/files/publications/magazines/bulletin/bull22-2/22204763445.pdf

5. Rosatom Oversea, The VVER today http://www.rosatom.ru/upload/iblock/0be/0be1220af25741375138ecd1afb18743.pdf

6. L. Kotchetkov, Obninsk: number one, https://www.neimagazine.com/features/featureobninsk-number-one/

7. World Nuclear Association, Nuclear Development in the United Kingdom, http://www.world-nuclear.org/information-library/country-profiles/countries-t-z/appendices/nuclear-development-in-the-united-kingdom.aspx#ECSArticleLink3

8. Queen Elizabeth II opening Calder Hall, https://www.youtube.com/watch?v=HNRz1FbXEek

9. Herbert L. Anderson, The Legacy of Fermi and Szilard, Bulletin of Atomic Scientists, Sept 1974, https://library.ucsd.edu/dc/object/bb52575421/_1.pdf

10. US NRC, Uranium Enrichment, https://www.nrc.gov/materials/fuel-cycle-fac/ur-enrichment.html

11. Joint Publications Research Service (JPRS), Nuclear development and proliferation. Chernobyl, https://www.cia.gov/library/readingroom/docs/CIA-RDP09-00997R000100270001-9.pdf

12. Nuclear Energy Agency, Chernobyl: Assessment of Radiological and Health Impact 2002 Update of Chernobyl: Ten Years On, https://www.oecd-nea.org/rp/chernobyl/c01.html

13. IAEA, The Chernobyl Accident: Updating of INSAG-1, A Report by the International Nuclear Safety Advisory Group, https://www-pub.iaea.org/books/iaeabooks/3786/The-Chernobyl-Accident-Updating-of-INSAG-11

14. IAEA, International Nuclear Safety Group (INSAG), https://www.iaea.org/topics/nuclear-safety-and-security/committees/insag

15. European Nuclear Society, What is a nuclear reactor?
    https://www.euronuclear.org/1-information/energy-uses.htm
16. Wikipedia, Rankine cycle, https://en.wikipedia.org/wiki/Rankine_cycle.
17. Nature's Nuclear Reactors: The 2-Billion-Year-Old Natural Fission Reactors in
    Gabon, Western Africa, https://blogs.scientificamerican.com/guest-blog/natures-
    nuclear-reactors-the-2-billion-year-old-natural-fission-reactors-in-gabon-
    western-africa/
18. World Nuclear Association, Nuclear Power Reactors, http://www.world-
    nuclear.org/information-library/nuclear-fuel-cycle/nuclear-power-
    reactors/nuclear-power-reactors.aspx
19. IAEA, Nuclear Power Reactors in the World, 2018,
    https://www.iaea.org/publications/13379/nuclear-power-reactors-in-the-world
20. IAEA, Safety Reports Series No. 43, Accident Analysis for Nuclear Power Plants
    with Graphite Moderated Boiling Water RBMK Reactors, http://www-
    pub.iaea.org/MTCD/publications/PDF/Pub1211_web.pdf.
21. U.S. Department of Energy, Office of Scientific and Technical Information,
    Russian RBMK reactor design information,
    http://www.osti.gov/bridge/servlets/purl/10194721-
    aGK72B/webviewable/10194721.pdf
22. T. Wellock, Putting the Axe to the 'Scram' Myth, https://public-blog.nrc-
    gateway.gov/2011/05/17/putting-the-axe-to-the-scram-myth/
23. C. Parisi, Nuclear Safety Of RBMK Reactors, PhD Thesis,
    https://core.ac.uk/download/pdf/14696543.pdf
24. B. Negus & W. S. Black, Winfrith SGHWR operating experiences 1968-1981, Nucl.
    Energy, 1981, Vol. 20, Oct., No. 5, 347-358 https://senior.app.box.com/BNES-
    VOL20-5 P.347
25. US Nuclear Regulatory Commission, Boiling Water Reactors,
    https://www.nrc.gov/reactors/bwrs.html.
26. New York Times, Design Flaws, Known To Moscow, Called Major Factor At
    Chernobyl, AUG. 26, 1986, https://www.nytimes.com/1986/08/26/world/design-
    flaws-known-to-moscow-called-major-factor-at-chernobyl.html
27. Reinterpreting Chernobyl, Nuclear Engineering International, 6 December 2017,
    https://www.neimagazine.com/features/featurereinterpreting-chernobyl-
    5991960/
28. WNA, Sequence of Events, Chernobyl Accident Appendix 1 *http://www.world-
    nuclear.org/information-library/safety-and-security/safety-of-
    plants/appendices/chernobyl-accident-appendix-1-sequence-of-events.aspx*
29. USSR State Committee on the Utilization of Atomic Energy, the Accident at the
    Chernobyl Nuclear Power Plant and its Consequences: Information Compiled for
    the IAEA Experts Meeting, 25-29 August 1986, Vienna Part I. General Material

https://www.iaea.org/inis/collection/NCLCollectionStore/_Public/18/001/18001971.pdf

30. A. Dyatlov, Why INSAG has still got it wrong, Nuclear Engineering International, September 1995, *http://www.neimagazine.com/features/featurewhy-insag-has-still-got-it-wrong*)

31. A. Dyatlov, How it was: an operator's perspective, Nuclear Engineering International, 19 April 2006, https://www.neimagazine.com/features/featurehow-it-was-an-operator-s-perspective/

32. Mikhail V. Malko, The Chernobyl Reactor: Design Features and Reasons for Accident, http://www.rri.kyoto-u.ac.jp/NSRG/reports/kr79/kr79pdf/Malko1.pdf

33. F. Motte, Reactor Division SCK/CEN, The Chernobyl-4 Reactor and the Possible Causes of the Accident, presented at the Seminar, The Chernobyl Accident and its Impact, organized by SCK/CEN at Mol, on October 7th 1986

34. J. Mahaffey, Atomic accidents, A history of nuclear meltdowns and disasters from the Ozark mountains to Fukushima. Pegasus Books, ISBN 978-1-60598-680-7.

35. S. Plokhy, *Chernobyl, history of a tragedy,* Allen Lane, ISBN 978-0-241-34902-1.

36. A. Leatherbarrow, Chernobyl 01:23:40, ISBN 9780993597503, 2016.

37. G.Medvedev (E. Rossiter translator), The Truth About Chernobyl, Basic Books, 1986. ISBN 0-465-08775-2

38. A. Higginbotham, Midnight in Chernobyl, The untold Story of the World's Greatest Nuclear Disaster, Bantam Press, ISBN 9780593076835, 2019.

39. IAEA, Summary Report on the Post-accident Review Meeting on the Chernobyl Accident, A Report by the International Nuclear Safety Advisory Group https://www-pub.iaea.org/books/iaeabooks/3598/Summary-Report-on-the-Post-accident-Review-Meeting-on-the-Chernobyl-Accident

40. Nuclear Data Center at KAERI, http://atom.kaeri.re.kr/nuchart/

41. The Chemogenesis web book, The Segré Chart, https://www.meta-synthesis.com/webbook/33_segre/segre.html

42. *Dominique Greneche, A nuclear Reactor, How it Works,* *http://www.jaif.or.jp/ja/wnu_si_intro/document/2012/5.3-6%20Dominique%20Greneche_A%20Nuclear%20Reactor%20how%20it%20works.pdf*

43. Encyclopædia Britannica, 2013, https://www.britannica.com/science/radioactivity/media/489089/19492

44. Physics of Uranium and Nuclear Energy, World Nuclear Association, 2018, http://www.world-nuclear.org/information-library/nuclear-fuel-cycle/introduction/physics-of-nuclear-energy.aspx

45. WIMS Library Update Project, IAEA, https://www-nds.iaea.org/wimsd/fpyield.htm

46. Wikipedia, Four factor formula, https://en.wikipedia.org/wiki/Four_factor_formula

47. Nuclear Power. Web. Operational factors that affect the multiplication in PWRs, https://www.nuclear-power.net/nuclear-power/reactor-physics/nuclear-fission-chain-reaction/operational-factors/

48. P Gulshani, A.R. Dastur, and B. Chexal, Stability Analysis Of Spatial Power Distribution In RBMK-1000 Reactor, http://www.iaea.org/inis/collection/NCLCollectionStore/_Public/20/052/20052963.pdf

49. John Wheeler's Interview (1965), https://www.manhattanprojectvoices.org/oral-histories/john-wheelers-interview-1965

50. M. Hyland, Risley (United Kingdom Atomic Energy Authority) Reactivity Coefficients in Nuclear Reactors, in Europhysics News, Nov/Dec 1987, https://www.europhysicsnews.org/articles/epn/pdf/1987/11/epn19871811p133.pdf

51. NUREG- 1250, "Report on the Accident at the Chernobyl Nuclear Power Station. https://www.nrc.gov/docs/ML0716/ML071690245.html

52. IAEA, Live chart of the nuclides, https://www-nds.iaea.org/relnsd/vcharthtml/VChartHTML.html

53. IAEA, Physics and Kinetics of TRIGA Reactors, https://ansn.iaea.org/Common/documents/Training/TRIGA%20Reactors%20(Safety%20and%20Technology)/chapter2/physics213.htm

54. U.S. Department of Energy, Office of Scientific and Technical Information, Evaluation and application of delayed neutron precursor data, https://www.osti.gov/servlets/purl/6187550

55. World Nuclear Association, Mixed Oxide (MOX) Fuel, http://www.world-nuclear.org/information-library/nuclear-fuel-cycle/fuel-recycling/mixed-oxide-fuel-mox.aspx

56. Gridwatch, 10:30 4/3/2019, http://gridwatch.co.uk/

57. C. D. Moak , The Xenon Culprit and Other Tales, in the Oak Ridge National Laboratory Review. https://www.ornl.gov/sites/default/files/ORNL%20Review%20v9n4%201976.pdf

58. Voices of the Manhattan Project, John Wheeler's Interview (1965), https://www.manhattanprojectvoices.org/oral-histories/john-wheelers-interview-1965

59. IAEA, Table of cumulative fission fragment yields, https://www-nds.iaea.org/sgnucdat/c3.htm

60. Canadian Nuclear Safety Commission, Technical Training Group, Science and Reactor Fundamentals, Reactor Physics, https://canteach.candu.org/Content%20Library/20030101.pdf

61. P.S.W. Chan et al, Multidimensional Analysis of the Chernobyl Accident, AECL-9604, 1988.

http://www.iaea.org/inis/collection/NCLCollectionStore/_Public/22/069/2206956
4.pdf

62. Nuclear Power, Diffusion Equation – Finite Cylindrical Reactor,
https://www.nuclear-power.net/nuclear-power/reactor-physics/neutron-
diffusion-theory/finite-cylindrical-reactor/

63. L. Lederman, IAEA, The Safety of RBMK Reactors 10 Years After Chernobyl,
http://www.iaea.org/inis/collection/NCLCollectionStore/_Public/28/023/2802379
8.pdf

64. Nosa, Mikael: RBMK simulator, https://www.theseus.fi/NOSA, MIKAEL: RBMK
simulator/10024/57937/Nosa_Mikael.pdf?sequence=1

65. Nuclear Power. Web, Two-phase Fluid Flow, https://www.nuclear-
power.net/nuclear-engineering/fluid-dynamics/two-phase-fluid-flow/

66. Rotech. All You Need To Know About Cavitation In Centrifugal Pumps,
https://www.rotechpumps.com/all-you-need-to-know-about-cavitation-in-
centrifugal-pumps

67. Nuclear Engineering International, Chernobyl, 26 April 1986,
https://www.neimagazine.com/features/featurechernobyl-26-april-1986/

68. C. Woodford, Steam Turbines, https://www.explainthatstuff.com/steam-
turbines.html

69. US-NCR, Glossary, https://www.nrc.gov/reading-rm/basic-ref/glossary/void-
coefficient-of-reactivity.html

70. Dmitriev Victor Markovich, The causes of Chernobyl accident are known,
http://accidont.ru/ENG/regul1.html

71. Gorbachev, B.I. The Causes and Scenario of the Chernobyl Accident and
Radioactive Release on the CHNPP Unit-4 Site. http://www.rri.kyoto-
u.ac.jp/NSRG/reports/kr79/kr79pdf/Gorbachev.pdf

72. E.O. Adamov et al, Chernobyl Accident Causes: Overview of Studies over the
Decade, in IAEA International Conference, One Decade After Chernobyl: Nuclear
Safety Aspects,
http://www.iaea.org/inis/collection/NCLCollectionStore/_Public/28/053/2805374
9.pdf

73. F. Reisch, Reactor Physics Behind the Chernobyl Accident,
http://www.iaea.org/inis/collection/NCLCollectionStore/_Public/31/049/3104955
0.pdf?r=1

74. T. Imanaka (editor), Recent Research Activities about the Chernobyl NPP
Accident in Belarus, Ukraine and Russia, http://www.rri.kyoto-
u.ac.jp/PUB/report/04_kr/img/ekr010.pdf

75. Chernobyl, DVD, Writer C. Mazin, Director J. Renck, A Sky original programme in
association with HBO. 2019.

76. World Nuclear News, Russia completes upgrade of third Smolensk RBMK, http://www.world-nuclear-news.org/Articles/Russia-completes-upgrade-of-third-Smolensk-RBMK

77. President of Ukraine Decree № 1156/2008, https://zakon.rada.gov.ua/laws/file/1156/2008

78. Wikipedia, Chernobyl Nuclear Power Plant sarcophagus, https://en.wikipedia.org/wiki/Chernobyl_Nuclear_Power_Plant_sarcophagus#CITEREFEbel1994

79. Wikipedia, Chernobyl New Safe Confinement, https://en.wikipedia.org/wiki/Chernobyl_New_Safe_Confinement

80. World Nuclear News, Chernobyl confinement structure systems begin operation, http://world-nuclear-news.org/Articles/Chernobyl-confinement-structure-systems-begin-oper

81. Chernobyl Trials, http://chernobylplace.com/chernobyl-trials/

82. J.T.Rogers, Insights from Chernobyl on Severe Accident Assessment of CANDU Reactors, https://canteach.candu.org/Content%20Library/NJC-1-2-03.pdf

83. Nikolai N. Ponomarev-Stepnoi, quoted in: Fifteenth Water Reactor Safety Information Meeting, Nuclear Safety, Vol. 29, No. 3, July-September 1988, https://www.osti.gov/scitech/servlets/purl/6808680

84. World Nuclear Association, Chernobyl Accident 1986, http://www.world-nuclear.org/information-library/safety-and-security/safety-of-plants/chernobyl-accident.aspx

85. Lord James Douglas-Hamilton, Hansard, https://api.parliament.uk/historic-hansard/commons/1987/mar/24/nuclear-power

86. IAEA, Lessons Learned from the Response to Radiation Emergencies (1945 - 2010), EPR-Lessons Learned 2012. https://www.iaea.org/publications/8920/lessons-learned-from-the-response-to-radiation-emergencies-1945-2010

87. N. V. Karpan, Analysis of the Version "Earthquake is the Cause of the Chernobyl Accident", http://www.rri.kyoto-u.ac.jp/NSRG/reports/kr139/pdf/karpan.pdf

88. K. Checherov, A different view on Chernobyl, http://commondms.digitalinsightresearch.in/Uploads/NewsArticle/5991960/d42fdd31-b740-48b4-962e-f621fb248ed6.pdf

89. De Geer, Persson & Rodhe, A Nuclear Jet at Chernobyl Around 21:23:45 UTC on April 25, 1986, https://www.tandfonline.com/doi/full/10.1080/00295450.2017.1384269?scroll=top&needAccess=true

90. Evangeliou, N., Hamburger, T., Cozic, A., Balkanski, Y., and Stohl, A.: Inverse 122odelling of the Chernobyl source term using atmospheric concentration and deposition measurements, Atmos. Chem. Phys., 17, 8805-8824,

https://doi.org/10.5194/acp-17-8805-2017, 2017. https://www.atmos-chem-phys.net/17/8805/2017/

91. BBC Wales, Chernobyl sheep controls lifted in Wales and Cumbria, https://www.bbc.co.uk/news/uk-wales-17472698

92. Met. Office, Chernobyl dispersion. https://metofficenews.files.wordpress.com/2011/04/chernobylcaesium-600.gif

93. F. A. Fry, R. H. Clarke & M. C. O'Riordan, Early estimates of UK radiation doses from the Chernobyl reactor, Nature volume 321, pages193–195 (1986), https://www.nature.com/articles/321193a0

94. M. Peplow, Special Report: Counting the dead, Nature volume 440, pages 982–983 (2006), https://www.nature.com/articles/440982a

95. The Chernobyl accident, UNSCEAR's assessments of the radiation effectsUnited Nations Scientific Committee on the Effects of Atomic Radiation (UNSCEAR), http://www.unscear.org/unscear/en/chernobyl.html

96. PHE, Ionising Radiation and you, https://www.phe-protectionservices.org.uk/radiationandyou/

97. Ionising Radiations Regulations 2017, https://www.legislation.gov.uk/uksi/2017/1075/schedule/3/made

98. Mind Tools, Root Cause Analysis Tracing a Problem to Its Origins. https://www.mindtools.com/pages/article/newTMC_80.htm

99. IAEA, Root Cause Analysis Following an Event at a Nuclear Installation: Reference Manual, IAEA-TECDOC-1756; (ISBN:978-92-0-110014-6); https://www-pub.iaea.org/books/iaeabooks/10626/Root-Cause-Analysis-Following-an-Event-at-a-Nuclear-Installation-Reference-Manual

100. WANO Peer Assist, https://www.wano.info/Web/files/14/146a3717-acb1-4ee2-9329-c1be1fb550f9.jpg

101. Nuclear Lessons Learned, The Royal Academy of Engineering, ISBN 1-903496-60-8 October 2010

102. IAEA, INSAG-12, Basic Safety Principles for Nuclear Power Plants 75-INSAG-3 Rev. 1, http://www-pub.iaea.org/MTCD/publications/PDF/P082_scr.pdf

103. James Reason, Human error: models and management, https://www.ncbi.nlm.nih.gov/pmc/articles/PMC1117770/

104. ONR, Events report published, http://news.onr.org.uk/2019/03/event-report-published/

105. LibreTexts, The Rydberg Formula and the Hydrogen Atomic Spectrum, https://chem.libretexts.org/Bookshelves/Physical_and_Theoretical_Chemistry_Textbook_Maps/Map%3A_Physical_Chemistry_(McQuarrie_and_Simon)/01%3A_The_Dawn_of_the_Quantum_Theory/1.5%3A_The_Rydberg_Formula_and_the_Hydrogen_Atomic_Spectrum

106. The Physics Hypertext Book, Photoelectric Effect, https://physics.info/photoelectric/

107. Nuclear Power Net, Ultraviolet Catastrophe – Rayleigh-Jeans Catastrophe, https://www.nuclear-power.net/nuclear-engineering/heat-transfer/radiation-heat-transfer/ultraviolet-catastrophe-rayleigh-jeans-catastrophe/

108. Hyperphysics, Wave Particle Duality, http://hyperphysics.phy-astr.gsu.edu/hbase/mod1.html

109. Louis-Victor de Broglie (1892-1987), On the Theory of Quanta, http://aflb.ensmp.fr/LDB-oeuvres/De_Broglie_Kracklauer.pdf

110. Schrödinger's cat, Wikipedia, https://en.wikipedia.org/wiki/Schr%C3%B6dinger%27s_cat

111. Libretexts, The Valley of Stability: Predicting the Type of Radioactivity, https://chem.libretexts.org/Textbook_Maps/General_Chemistry/Map%3A_A_Molecular_Approach_(Tro)/20%3A_Radioactivity_and_Nuclear_Chemistry/20.04%3A_The_Valley_of_Stability%3A_Predicting_the_Type_of_Radioactivity

112. Hyperphysics, Electron Neutrinos and Antineutrinos, http://hyperphysics.phy-astr.gsu.edu/hbase/Particles/neutrino.html

113. Openstax, 21.1 Nuclear Structure and Stability https://opentextbc.ca/chemistry/chapter/21-1-nuclear-structure-and-stability/

114. Radioactivity.eu.com, β decay : weak forces http://www.radioactivity.eu.com/site/pages/Mechanism_beta_decay.htm

115. Fermi National Accelerator Laboratory, The weak force, https://home.fnal.gov/~cheung/rtes/RTESWeb/LQCD_site/pages/weakforce.htm

116. Hyperphysics, Transformation of Quark Flavors by the Weak Interaction http://hyperphysics.phy-astr.gsu.edu/hbase/Particles/qrkdec.html#c1

117. Jefferson lab, Beta decay, https://education.jlab.org/glossary/betadecay.html

118. Hyperphysics, Modeling Alpha Half-life http://hyperphysics.phy-astr.gsu.edu/hbase/Nuclear/alpdec.html

119. Imperial College HEP Research Group, Nuclear and Particle Physics - Lecture 22, Alpha decay http://www.hep.ph.ic.ac.uk/~dauncey/will/lecture22.pdf

120. Hyperphysics, Beta Radioactivity, http://hyperphysics.phy-astr.gsu.edu/hbase/Nuclear/beta.html

121. Hyperphysics, http ://hyperphysics.phy-astr.gsu.edu/hbase/Nuclear/radser.html

122. Nucleonica, Modes of radioactive decay, https://www.nucleonica.com/Application/KNC/Modes%20of%20Radioactive%20Decay.pdf

123. CGPM, On the revision of the International System of Units (SI) https://www.bipm.org/utils/en/pdf/CGPM/Draft-Resolution-A-EN.pdf

124. PIPM, On the revision of the SI https://www.bipm.org/en/measurement-units/rev-si/

125. Boston University Physics, Nuclear Binding Energy and the Mass Defect, http://physics.bu.edu/~duffy/sc546_notes10/mass_defect.html

126. M. Tanabashi et al. (Particle Data Group), Phys. Rev. D 98, 030001 (2018),
http://pdg.lbl.gov/2018/listings/rpp2018-list-p.pdf

127. M. Tanabashi et al. (Particle Data Group), Phys. Rev. D 98, 030001 (2018)
http://pdg.lbl.gov/2018/listings/rpp2018-list-n.pdf

128. Brookhaven National Laboratory, National Nuclear Data Center,
www.nndc.bnl.gov

129. Tables of Physical & Chemical Constants (16th edition 1995). Kaye & Laby Online.
Version 1.0 (2005) www.kayelaby.npl.co.uk

130. IAEA, Atomic Mass Adjustment, https://www-
nds.iaea.org/amdc/ame2016/mass16round.txt

131. Chinese Physics C Vol. 41, No. 3 (2017) 030003,
http://cms.iopscience.org/085e4ab8-0d63-11e7-9a47-
19ee90157113/030003_Table1.pdf?guest=true

132. Nuclear Power Net, Reactor Period, https://www.nuclear-power.net/nuclear-
power/reactor-physics/nuclear-fission-chain-reaction/reactivity/reactor-period-
2/

133. DOE Fundamentals Handbook Nuclear Physics and Reactor Theory, Volumes 1
and 2, http://www.nrcprep.com/home/references/DOEfundamentals

134. William Penney et al 2017, Report on the accident at Windscale No. 1 Pile on 10
October 1957, J. Radiol. Prot. 37 780,
https://iopscience.iop.org/article/10.1088/1361-6498/aa7788

135. Research Reactors, World Nuclear Association, https://world-
nuclear.org/information-library/non-power-nuclear-applications/radioisotopes-
research/research-reactors.aspx

136. Nuclear Energy Agency, Evaluated nuclear reaction data, http://www.oecd-
nea.org/dbdata/data/evaluated.htm

137. M. Ragheb, Decay heat generation in fission reactors, 2014.
https://mragheb.com/NPRE%20457%20CSE%20462%20Safety%20Analysis%20of
%20Nuclear%20Reactor%20Systems/Decay%20Heat%20generation%20in%20Fis
sion%20Reactors.pdf

138. Glasstone & Sesonski, Nuclear Reactor Engineering, Third edition, 1981, ISBN 0-
442-20057-9.

139. E.E.Lewis, Fundamentals of Nuclear Reactor Physics, 2008, ISBN 978-0-12-
370631-7.

Published by Katwab Limited, All rights reserved

ISBN 978-1-9164658-1-7

Also by Keith Pearce. Available as a paperback or Kindle book on Amazon

How to survive a nuclear emergency.

This book provides advice to members of the public about how to prepare for and respond to a nuclear emergency that sends a plume of radioactive materials over their homes or places or work (or just threatens to).

This book should be read by anyone who lives near a nuclear site or anyone interested in the potential impact of a nuclear emergency.

It shows how to prepare for, and how to respond to, a nuclear emergency (or many other types of emergency that may require you to leave your home at short notice).

With this information you should be able to better understand any advice being given by the authorities and be more confident about keeping your family and friends safe throughout the ordeal.

Nuclear Emergency Response for local authorities - An introduction

This book should be read by people who, although not nuclear industry specialists, may have to respond to an off-site nuclear emergency in some capacity. It gives:

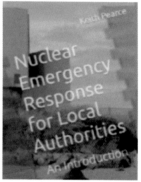

- an understanding of what a nuclear emergency is and its potential consequences; the operation and fault modes of the AGR class of reactors, and how these would be reported to the SCC. This is given in sufficient detail to allow those in the SCC to follow the discussions about the release prognosis;
- information on related events such as dirty bombs, orphan sources, nuclear satellite re-entry and nuclear bombs;
- an understanding of radiation protection covering the effects and risks of radiation, compared to everyday risks, as well as dose assessment and dose limitation;
- a review of the International Commission on Radiological Protection (ICRP) advice on communicating with the public on these matters;
- an outline of UK emergency planning including the challenges presented with informing and protecting the public in affected areas;
- an outline of countermeasures; how they work, how we (the industry) decide which ones to recommend and the decision making process within the SCC;
- a review of communicating within the SCC; who knows what and what does it mean?
- a decision process for work within affected areas;

Made in the USA
Middletown, DE
03 December 2019

79968959R00075